HOW WE KNOW

NOBEL CONFERENCE XX

Gustavus Adolphus College, St. Peter, Minnesota

HOW WE KNOW

Edited by
MICHAEL SHAFTO

With Contributions by
Gerald M. Edelman, Brenda Milner, Roger C. Schank,
Herbert A. Simon, Daniel Dennett,
and Arthur Peacocke

1817

Harper & Row, Publishers, San Francisco
Cambridge, Hagerstown, New York, Philadelphia
London, Mexico City, São Paulo, Singapore, Sydney

FIRST EDITION

Library of Congress Cataloging-in-Publication Data
Nobel Conference (20th : 1985 : Gustavus Adolphus College)
  How we know.
    1. Cognition—Congresses. 2. Artificial intellegence—Congresses. I. Shafto, Michael. II. Edelman, Gerald M. III. Title.
BF311.N62 1985   153   85-21871
ISBN 0-06-250777-X

---

85 86 87 88 89 HC 10 9 8 7 6 5 4 3 2 1

Contents

22930

Acknowledgments

The idea behind Nobel XX came from three membes of the Gustavus faculty: Drs. George Georgacarakos, John Holte, and Mark Kruger. The intellectual direction and scope of the conference were sharpened by Drs. Deborah Downs-Miers, Robert Esbjornson, David Fienen, John Kendall, Mark Lammers, Karen Larson, Timothy Robinson, Stanley Shetka, and James Welsh. Many other Gustavus students and faculty gave of their time and talents to make Nobel XX a celebration not only of the sciences, but also of the arts and humanities. The Gustavus staff, especially Elaine Brostrom, Dee Waldron, Jeanie Reese, Dennis Paschke, Dale Haack, and Linda Miller, were indispensable as always in making the conference a reality.

Of course there could have been no basis for the conference or this book without the several lifetimes of innovative research and thinking represented by the six principal contributors. In addition, over 3,000 students, educators, and members of the general public participated in Nobel XX. Their active involvement contributed to the air of exhilaration that pervaded the conference, and that involvement is reflected in the discussion questions at the end of each chapter in this volume.

Harper & Row is becoming a familiar and welcome friend of the Nobel Conference series. Ron Haxton was a constant source of enthusiasm and encouragement from the earliest planning stages of Nobel XX; Clayton Carlson, Dorian Gossy, Matt Chanoff, Melanie Haage, and their colleagues have worked intelligently and wisely to make this book a timely and useful overview of cognitive science.

The Introduction owes a great deal to Stephen Stich's recent book, *From Folk Psychology to Cognitive Science*, and also to the critical comments of Drs. Susan Chipman and Sylvia Shafto. Dr. Sylvia Shafto's combined expertise in biology and computer science was relied upon in the editing of the entire book.

Finally, special thanks are due to Dr. Edgar Carlson, who originated the idea of the Nobel Conference at Gustavus Adolphus College; to the Lund family for the endowment gift which has provided continuing financial support; to Chaplain Richard Elvee, who has intellectually sustained and strengthened the conference series in recent years; and to that inspirational trio from Nobel XXIII: Stephen Jay Gould, Sir Peter Medawar, and "Ham."

Introduction

There is nothing more disenchanting to man than to be shown the springs and mechanisms of any art. All our arts and occupations lie wholly on the surface; it is on the surface that we perceive their beauty, fitness, and significance; and to pry below is to be appalled by their emptiness and shocked by the coarseness of the strings and pulleys. In a similar way, psychology itself, when pushed to any nicety, discovers an abhorrent baldness, but rather from the fault of our analysis than from any poverty native to the mind. And perhaps in esthetics the reason is the same: those disclosures which seem fatal to the dignity of art, seem so perhaps only in the proportion of our ignorance; and those conscious and unconscious artifices which it seems unworthy of the serious artist to employ, were yet, if we had the power to trace them to their springs, indications of a delicacy of the sense finer than we conceive, and hints of ancient harmonies in nature.

—ROBERT LOUIS STEVENSON

The contributors to Nobel XX share science's commitment to seek out the springs and mechanisms, the strings and pulleys, behind nature's patiently contrived artifices. This commitment rests on the belief that imaginative attention to the details of behavior will earn a deep understanding of human nature. The scientific attitude toward human beings is not a naive reductionism, but rather a faith that our minds will be able to come into equilibrium with an ever-expanding range of phenomena, including those biological, psychological, and sociological phenomena closest to human concerns. We can strive, with some hope of success, toward Whitehead's ideal of a "coherent, logical, necessary system of general ideas in terms of which every element of our experience can be interpreted."

Common sense gives way grudgingly, especially in how we explain ourselves to ourselves. The mind is homeostatic, reverent of the status quo, even as it is attuned to and quickly captured by novelty. Delighted with the beauty, fitness, and significance of the play, it is not apt to peek backstage. With respect to the physical world, folk concepts and pseudoexplanations have given way to abstract theories encompassing spans of space-time and labyrinths of mathematics that baffle the nonspecialist. Cognitive science may produce similarly esoteric explanations of the mechanisms behind our own thoughts and feelings, and such explanations may eventually replace folk psychology as the true story of humans in nature. Is this prospect disenchanting, appalling, abhorrent?

The specialist's deep understanding of the physical world is not reflected in a particularly high level of understanding among the general populace. How many of us could win a debate against a clever opponent who was prepared to argue that the earth is flat, the sun revolves around it, and the whole universe was created from nothing in 4004 B.C.? How many of us can explain the principles of design and function of the refrigerator, the internal combustion engine, house plants, or the family dog? Cognitive science may well advance the specialist's understanding of intelligence without having much impact on the working assumptions of everyday life.

Even if cognitive science never increases the average person's insight into his or her own behavior, however, it may provide indirect benefit through its technological impact. Our respect for the physical sciences often derives not from their ability to make our world more comprehensible to us, but from their technological products—space flight, nuclear power, genetic engineering, air conditioning, microwave ovens, video games—the accessories that make us, in Freud's words, "prosthetic gods."

Significant technical and practical achievements are just beginning to emerge from cognitive science. We do not know what the future holds for computer vision, robotics, speech analysis and synthesis, natural language understanding, expert systems, and machine learning. The following speculations, written by Lynette Hirschman in *Ikon,* may not be far off the mark:

You will no longer have to pay an accountant to do taxes—you will just dial up an expert accounting program to help you. You will talk to this program in ordinary English (or Spanish, etc.), and the program will explain as much (or as little) of its reasoning as you wish to know. If you have a medical problem, you will dial up the medical diagnosis program; it will ask you about your symptoms and advise you about what to do. It will almost certainly be better at explaining things than most doctors. Similarly for legal problems, financial planning, vocational guidance, even vacation planning. Formerly esoteric, expensive expertise will become readily available to a very large part of the population at affordable prices.

The impact of the expert system is analogous to the impact of the printing press in the medieval period: it will lead to the demystification of expertise in many areas.

Certainly there are venture capitalists who share Hirschman's vision. At present, however, cognitive science is just taking shape. Its principal professional organization, the Cognitive Science Society, held only its seventh annual meeting in 1985. Almost all the leading pioneers of cognitive science are still actively developing their ideas and pursuing their research.

Although its philosophical origins date from the beginnings of philosophy itself, and its scientific origins can be found in the latter nineteenth century, cognitive science as a self-conscious coalition of thinkers is barely a decade old. It represents the discovery, by psychologists, philosophers, neuroscientists, linguists, anthropologists, and computer scientists, of a set of difficult questions about the formal and physical properties of intelligent systems. Part of the discovery of these questions was the realization that answering them (and even asking them) required crossing traditional disciplinary boundaries.

Given its interdisciplinary structure and the historical differences in perspective among its component disciplines, cognitive science may not survive at all. Its factual content comes from laboratory studies of perception, learning, memory, language, and reasoning. Its methods are those of experimental psychology, physiology, and computer science. Some of its key assumptions are that human cognition can be described in terms of functional limitations, such as memory capacity and processing speed; that the underlying principles of intelligent behavior can be understood mechanistically; and that some kinds of intelligence can be modeled on present-day digital computers. To common sense, these methods and assumptions may often seem strange or even irreverent.

There is a certain hybrid vigor to this new multidiscipline, but there are also disadvantages to its being built out of several permanent factions. There is the ever-present tendency for the physiologists to retreat to reductionism, the philosophers to formalism, the psychologists to operationalism, and the computer scientists to the private sector.

The concepts and theories of cognitive science are already alien to commonsense ideas about behavior and mental life. For example, a debate is under way among cognitive scientists regarding the relation of neurophysiology to cognition. (Perhaps this is a computer-age rendition of the mind-body problem.) The contributors to Nobel XX represent a variety of positions on this topic. The point, however, is that the issues in the debate are not accessible to common sense. They are technical issues, on a par with the kinds of issues that might divide warring factions of theoretical physicists. They have to do with abstract philosophical questions about the nature of explanation in psychological science. They have to do with the relation of the structure of a hypothetical computer to the time and space required to run various classes of programs on it. They have to do with the relation of the latest data from neurophysiological laboratories to the latest simulation running on the latest parallel computing architecture.

This does not mean that these issues are beyond the comprehension of nonspecialists. The main goal of Nobel XX and of this book is to show otherwise. It simply means that these issues cannot be debated in the language of common sense. Some technical concepts are needed.

Even though cognitive science seeks to explain how we know, how we think, how we perceive and believe, the scientist's conception of knowing, thinking, perceiving, and believing has already parted company with the familiar and comfortable folk concepts of everyday language. Familiar terms disappear or become unrecognizable, like the physicist's terms *force, power,* and *stress.*

If this sort of transformation annoys or disturbs you, or if it simply bores you, then you may be among the billions of healthy, normal people who are not destined to become cognitive scientists. The participants in Nobel XX, however, are unusual people. They are not content to let appearance be reality. They want to see the springs and strings and pulleys behind the scenes. For them, there is mystery in the familiar. A polished performance arouses as much suspicion as admiration. Simple, everyday acts like reading a book or recognizing a tune or telling a story seem to be near-miracles—but not *actual* miracles, because these everyday events can be explained once we see how strange and puzzling they are, and once we realize that they require explanation.

Gerald Edelman reminds us that biological systems have emerged from a universe that affords a rich substrate of possibilities. Human beings are part of this evolving universe. Biological intelligence shows the operation of selectionist mechanisms on a new, emergent level, a level that reflects the tangled thicket of possibilities from which it evolved and to which it must adapt in order to survive. The mechanisms behind the simplest adaptive behavior are subtle and convoluted. Introspection and folk psychology are poor guides: We simply do not know how we know. But cognitive scientists are human beings, and their theoretical language may lapse back into the folk idiom. The little man in the head, the homunculus, appears magically to do all the hard work: storing information away, retrieving it at the opportune moment, recognizing stimuli, selecting responses, and even making occasional errors. Homunculi are fatal to theories with scientific ambitions. Neurophysiologists exorcise homunculi, and Edelman is a master of the art.

Brenda Milner has led the way in exploring the neurophysiological basis of that critical moment when a new experience has its effect on the brain. Her work shows that what is special about us depends in unexpected ways on the details of our brain structure. Her insights have resulted from careful preparation, alertness to opportunity, and scrupulous scientific experimentation—not from introspection or metaphorical argument. Again, the springs and mechanisms are alien to common sense, and yet the accounts of HM and the others are as poignant and as moving as any poem or passage from literature. We see new aspects of human nature. If that is disenchanting, so be it.

Roger Schank and Colleen Seifert use an engaging series of examples to make a further point about that moment in which a new experience is first apprehended and interpreted. In intelligent systems new experiences are related (intelligently) to past experiences. They modify the interpretation of those remembered experiences. This is where the action is: at the interface between perception and memory. This is why human memory is dynamic, unlike the memory of the computer, and why the intelligent functions of memory are so difficult to implement on a computer. Explaining how the human brain updates its memory is a major unsolved problem for cognitive science, but even stating the problem cogently is an important achievement.

Herbert Simon articulates and illustrates the basic conceptual framework of cognitive science. This framework emphasizes levels of description, each of which reveals some of the truth about intelligence. He identifies a few simple principles that unite different types of intelligent systems (physical symbol systems). He emphasizes two ways to exorcise homunculi noninvasively: experimental studies of behavior and computer-based cognitive modeling. These methods, in the hands of Simon and his colleagues, have defined cognitive science and have made possible its most impressive achievements. The view of a person as a "subject" in a laboratory experiment and the notion of human intelligence as akin to a program in a computer do not fit well with common sense. Artificial intelligence seems a threat or a sham. To the cognitive scientist, however, the degree of similarity between humans and computers is an empirical question, a question to be answered by research rather than intuition.

Daniel Dennett, coming from the more speculative tradition of philosophy, suggests that the problem is not too much intuition but not enough. We need "intuition pumps" to help us see the myriad possibilities and plausibilities that are near to reality. By envisioning forms and states that have not existed, but could have and may yet exist, we can imagine and examine contrasts that might take millennia to find in the laboratory. Dennett shows us that we *can* exist in the universe as we know it, though perhaps not as we "know" ourselves. That is, intelligence does not require the circularities, inconsistencies, and magical ingredients of folk psychology. Intelligent systems can emerge (and so they have) from the same universe that physicists, chemists, and biologists study. There are innumerable possible types of intelligence, some of which are realized in animals, some in computer programs, some in human beings, and the vast majority not at all. Dennett also shows us that there is a world of difference between introspection and reflection. The former is inimical to cognitive science; the latter is essential to it.

Arthur Peacocke brings to Nobel XX not only superb credentials in biology, chemistry, and theology, but also the ability to listen with his whole mind. Like Edelman, Simon, and Dennett, he touches on the themes of levels and of possibility. As we reflect on our humanity within the mechanistic framework of cognitive science, we initially find nothing special in us to set us apart from the universe. We are invited, however, to reflect further: There is something special about the universe itself, namely, its richness of possibilities (one of which is us). And then we begin to sense something unexpectedly special about ourselves.

The beauty, fitness, and significance of our minds at their best is experienced immediately as subjective awareness of the world, or almost immediately through empathy and communication with other minds. Though they nourish rather than compete with science, perceptual experience and the effortless energy of common sense will always outdance the clanking mechanisms of cognitive science.

We may hope that the abhorrent baldness of physiological mechanisms or rule-based computational models are simply the fault of our present analysis. But it is perhaps indicative of another truth that, among the contributors to Nobel XX, in every case the scientist is a humanist after all. These six scientists show by personal example that discoveries and speculations about the mechanisms of our own brains and minds need not be fatal to our dignity. Rather, as our ignorance is reduced, we realize more clearly that the mechanisms beneath the surface of mental life lie on the surface of a deeper reality. Discoveries on the inner frontier of cognitive science complement discoveries in the other sciences, contributing a few more fragments of melody that allow us to sense ancient harmonies in nature.

Michael G. Shafto
Falls Church, Virginia
June 11, 1985

Contributors

Gerald M. Edelman received his B.S. degree from Ursinus College, Collegeville, Pennsylvania, his M.D. from the University of Pennsylvania, and his Ph.D. from Rockefeller University. He has been Vincent Astor Distinguished Professor at the Rockefeller University since 1974, and Director and Scientific Chairman of the Neurosciences Research Program since 1981. He received the Nobel Prize in medicine and physiology in 1972 for his research into the molecular structure of immunoglobin, which led to a broader understanding of the biochemistry of the human immune system. In 1974 he received the Albert Einstein Commemorative Award. He is a fellow of the National Academy of Sciences, the American Academy of Arts and Sciences, and the American Association for the Advancement of Science. With Vernon Mountcastle, he is the co-author of *The Mindful Brain*.

Brenda Milner was born in England and educated at Cambridge University, where she worked with Sir Frederic Bartlett, one of the pioneers in cognitive research on learning and memory. She is currently Professor of Psychology in the Department of Neurology and Neurosurgery, McGill University, and head of the Neuropsychology Laboratory, Montreal Neurological Institute and Hospital. She received the Stott Prize for Scientific Research from Newnham College, Cambridge, in 1971 and the Distinguished Scientific Contribution Award from the American Psychological Association in 1973. She is a fellow of the Royal Society of Canada, the American Psychological Association, and the American Association for the Advancement of Science. She is author of *Brain Function and Cognition*.

Roger C. Schank is Professor and Chairman of the Computer Science Department, Professor of Psychology, and Director of the Artificial Intelligence Project at Yale University. He is a member of the governing board of the Cognitive Science Society and is on the editorial boards of the journals *Cognitive Science* and *Behavioral and Brain Sciences.* He is the author or co-author of numerous books, including *Conceptual Information Processing; Scripts, Plans, Goals, and Understanding; Reading and Understanding: Teaching from an Artificial Intelligence Perspective;* and *Dynamic Memory.*

Colleen M. Seifert is a graduate student in the Cognitive Science Program at Yale University. As an undergraduate psychology major at Gustavus Adolphus College, she studied cognitive psychology with Michael Shafto, who introduced her to Roger Schank's work. For her outstanding achievements in both experimental and clinical psychology, she received the 1980 Donald G. Paterson Award from the Minnesota State Psychological Association. Since 1980 she has been studying psychology and artificial intelligence with Schank and others at Yale. Her current research is focused on the process of seeking and interpreting advice in everyday situations.

Herbert A. Simon is Richard King Mellon University Professor of Computer Science and Psychology at Carnegie-Mellon University. He is a member of the American Association for Artificial Intelligence, the American Philosophical Society, and the National Academy of Sciences. He received the Nobel Memorial Prize in Economic Science in 1978 for his pioneering research into the decision-making processes within economic organizations. He has held academic and administrative positions at the University of California, Berkeley, Illinois Institute of Technology, and Carnegie-Mellon University, in departments of Political Science, Industrial Management, Psychology, and Computer Science. He has received the Distinguished Scientific Contribution Award of the American Psychological Association, the A. M. Turing Award of the Association for Computing Machinery, and election as a Distinguished Fellow of the American Economic Association. He is the author or co-author of numerous articles and books, including *Administrative Behavior, Models of Discovery, Models of Thought, The Sciences of the Artificial,* and *Reason in Human Affairs.*

Daniel C. Dennett is Professor of Philosophy at Tufts University. He held Santayana and NEH Younger Humanist Fellowships at Harvard in 1974. He was a Fulbright Fellow at the University of Bristol in 1978, NEH Humanities Senior Fellow in 1979, and John Locke Lecturer at Oxford University in 1983. He is Associate Editor of *Behavioral and Brain Sciences*; author of *Content and Consciousness, Brainstorms: Philosophical Essays on Mind and Psychology,* and *Elbow Room: The Varieties of Free Will Worth Wanting*; and co-editor with Douglas Hofstadter of *The Mind's I: Fantasies and Reflections on Self and Soul.*

Arthur R. Peacocke is Director of the Ian Ramsey Center for the study of ethical problems, St. Cross College, Oxford. Before accepting this position, he was Dean of Clare College, Cambridge University. He serves as an associate editor of *Zygon,* a journal of religion and science. In 1973 he received the International Lecomte du Nouy Prize for his book *Science and the Christian Experiment.* He is also the author of *From Cosmos to Love: The Meaning of Human Life, Creation and the World of Science,* and *An Introduction to the Physical Chemistry of Biological Organization.*

Michael G. Shafto is a Scientific Officer in the Personnel and Training Research Programs, U.S. Office of Naval Research. He received his Ph.D. from Princeton University in 1974, where his research was primarily concerned with psycholinguistics. He received the James McKeen Cattell Award of the New York Academy of Sciences and the Distinguished Service Award of the New Jersey State Psychological Association for his research at Princeton. From 1974 to 1984 he taught cognitive psychology and related topics at Gustavus Adolphus College. His teaching and research efforts during this period were supported by the Minnesota Educational Computing Consortium, the Paul and Mary Chelgren Fund, the National Science Foundation, the Sloan Foundation, and the Woodrow Wilson Foundation.

1. Neural Darwinism: Population Thinking and Higher Brain Function

GERALD M. EDELMAN

My remarks shall be about the greatest inner frontier of present-day science, the nature and functions of the human brain. I want to convey some of the excitement of working on this subject. But I want also to convey some sense of the theoretical crises, for it is in recognizing these that we know we are at the frontier. I will suggest a population theory of the brain that has as its major goal the resolution of these crises. Before I do that, I must point to a curious gap that has always plagued psychology.

This gap has to do with the inability to match global or functional descriptions of behavior with structural descriptions of the brain. No one will deny the blatant truism that the brain is necessary to cognitive function. Nonetheless, a scholar searching the literature of modern cognitive psychology and of that hopeful monster, artificial intelligence, will be hard-pressed to find the brain a central concern. Although this curious absence is not necessarily a defect, it is certainly a limitation: Questions may be formulated at a level where they are not decidable, or models may depend excessively upon so-called top-down, linguistically based analyses. Above all, certain fundamental methodological issues, such as the nature of categorization and generalization, may be skirted, particularly in formulating theories of learning and memory.

On the other side, brain scientists often simply ignore cognitive issues as being too removed from their true concerns. Worse yet,

This work was supported by U.S. Public Health Service Grants AM-04256, HD-09635, and a grant from the IBM Corporation.

they may tacitly accept certain ways of thinking about cognition itself that have curious resemblances to engineering theories applicable to the instruments they use in their research. The brain as a computer or an information-processing machine is certainly a frequently encountered metaphor.

Both these positions may be defended on the grounds that the gap between brain structure and function and psychology is still too wide to be bridged. But there may be some value, nonetheless, in taking the position that what is lacking on either side is not more data but an adequate theory of higher brain function. Such a theory cannot be derived solely from neuroanatomy, neurophysiology, or psychology. As I have already suggested, it must start by confronting some crises that have arisen in a variety of fields of neurobiology and by attempting to resolve them, which amounts to showing how they are linked.

In considering these crises, I want to suggest a view of the brain and its function that differs radically from those currently accepted. The view is that, in its function, the brain is Darwinian: neural circuits and groups of neurons form populations consisting of variant individuals. During ontogeny and behavior, selection is made from these populations of those groups of neurons that are adaptive for the organism. I shall describe this view as it is embodied in the so-called theory of neuronal group selection.[1] Baldly stated here, and before considering the various crises of neuroscience, it is not apparent that this theory has any advantage over any other. To show that it does, I will first turn to a brief description of these crises and only afterward state the theory in greater detail. Then I can consider some salient evidence in support of this notion of neural Darwinism.

THE CRISES OF NEUROSCIENCE

The brain in complex animals, such as human beings, consists of sheets, or laminae, and of more or less rounded structures called nuclei. Each of these structures has evolved to carry out functions in a complex network of connections, and each consists of very large numbers of neurons. The connection to the outside world is by means of specialized neurons called sensory transducers, which make up sense organs; this is the input to the brain. The output is by means of neurons to muscles and glands. In addition, parts of the brain (indeed, the major portion of its tissue) receive input only from other parts, and they give outputs to other parts without intervention from the outside.[2]

How do neurons connect with each other, and how are they arranged within nuclei and laminae? The major means of connection is via the synapse, a specialized structure in which electrical activity passed down the axon of the presynaptic neuron (fig. 1) leads to release of a chemical (neurotransmitter) that in turn induces electrical activity in the postsynaptic neuron. Neurons themselves can be arranged in a variety of complex ways but are sometimes disposed into maps. An example is the correspondence of portions of the cerebral cortex responsive to light touch on the skin to the order of the skin on different body parts (see fig. 5 for an example). This type of mapping is called somatotopy.

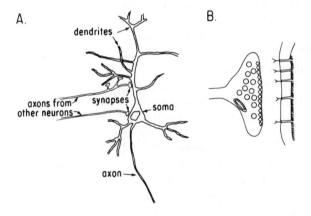

Figure 1. Diagrams of neurons in circuits and of synapses. *A.* Axons from near or distant neurons make contact with a neuron either on its body (soma) or on its branching processes, called dendrites. Axons carry electrical activity that when it reaches a synapse can release a neurotransmitter. This in turn can trigger the recipient neuron (or postsynaptic neuron) to fire electrically. *B.* A synapse. The circles in the structure on the left represent vesicles containing neurotransmitter in the presynaptic neuron. The postsynaptic neuron projects receptors (the **y**-shaped structures) into the cleft between the pre- and postsynaptic membranes. These receptors bind transmitter released from the presynaptic vesicles. For further details, see notes 2 and 3.

So far, what I have described in a brief and coarse fashion sounds very much like the organization of a vast telephone exchange or even like that of a digital computer. Indeed, in many ways the system behaves like these structures. But when we look at certain detailed structural features and certain functional behaviors of the nervous system, the analogy breaks down, and we confront crisis.

I shall give several examples of structural and functional crises, knowing that the precision of my remarks will suffer because I am addressing a general intelligent audience and not a group of specialists. With each example, I will try to explain away the crisis using what I believe to be the accepted position in each area to which the crisis pertains. Obviously, I consider these explanations unsatisfactory and hope to provide more satisfactory alternatives when I get to explaining population theories of the brain.

The structural crises are those of anatomy and development.[3] Although the brain looks like a vast electrical network at one level, at its most microscopic level it is not connected or arranged like any other known or man-made network.[4] The network of the brain is made during development by cellular movements, extensions, and connections of increasing numbers of neurons. It is an example of a self-organizing system. An examination of such a system during its development and at its most microscopic ramifications after development indicates that precise point-to-point wiring cannot occur. Therefore, uniquely specific connections cannot, in general, exist. If one numbered the branches of a neuron and correspondingly numbered the neurons it touched, the numbers would not correspond in any two individuals of a species (even in identical twins or in genetically identical animals).

To make matters worse, neurons generally send branches of their axons out in diverging arbors overlapping with those of other neurons, and the same is true of certain processes (called dendrites) on recipient neurons. The point is that, if we asked a particular neuron which input came from which other neuron in the overlapping set of connections, it could not "know."

The existence of principles of development that lead to variance in connections, and of overlapping arbors with unidentifiable (and not necessarily repeatable) patterns of synapses, constitutes a crisis for those who believe that the nervous system is precise and "hard-wired" (like a computer). How is this crisis met by conventional explanations, if it is recognized at all?

First, variations below a certain microscopic level are considered to be "noise," a necessary consequence of the developmental dilemma. Second, the absence of uniquely specific connections is treated by arguing that higher levels of organization, or maps, either do not need such connections or compensate for their absence in some fashion. And the absence of anatomically identified synaptic inputs can be dealt with by assuming that neurons use a code much in the same way that codes can be exploited to identify phone credit card users or computer users. Of course, in neurons, the presumed codes would relate to the frequency, spacing, or type of their electrical activity or to the particular chemical transmitters with which they are associated. Notice that all these explanations assume that individual neurons carry information just as certain electronic devices carry information. I shall argue later that this is not a defensible assumption and that these explanations are inadequate.

Before I do so, however, let me turn to what I shall label functional crises, pertaining more to physiology and psychology. The first of these is that if one explores the microscopic network of synapses with electrodes, the majority of them are not expressed, that is, they show no detectable activity. They are what have been called silent synapses. But why are they silent, and how does their silence relate to the signals, codes, or messages that *are* supposed to be expressed?

A more striking dilemma, to which I shall revert later in an extensive discussion, concerns maps. Despite the conventional wisdom of anatomy books, there are major temporal fluctuations in the borders of maps in some brain laminae. Moreover, maps in each different individual appear to be unique. Most strikingly, the variability of maps in adult animals depends upon the available input. This does not seem a dilemma at first; after all, computers can change their "maps" upon alteration of software. But the maps of the nervous system are based on anatomic maps—at this level they are only changed in the adult brain by death of neurons. If these maps are changing as a result of "software" changes, what is the code that can give two different individuals with variant maps the same output or result? One conventional explanation is to say that there are alternative systems in the brain that can handle changing input, each alternative fixed and hard-wired but switched differently by changing input. As we shall see, however, the facts show that the variance of maps is not discrete or two-valued but continuous, fine-grained, and, at the same time, extensive.

The next two crises bring us closer to psychological dilemmas of the most profound kind. The first casts doubt on the idea that complex behavior of animals with complex brains can be explained solely by learning. Indeed, I believe it highlights the most fundamental problem of neuroscience: How can an animal confront a small number of events or "objects" and, after such exposure, adaptively categorize or recognize an indefinite number of novel objects in a variety of contexts as being similar or identical to the set that it first encountered? Put briefly, how can an animal recognize an object at all? How can it then generalize and "construct a universal" in the absence of that object, or even in its presence? The fact is that this kind of generalization can occur in pigeons, without language, as I shall discuss later. Usually explanations of this profoundly challenging problem rely upon the existence of hidden cues not obvious to the experimenter, or they treat the world of the responding organism as if its "objects" or "events" came with labels on them.

The final crisis I earmark here will no doubt be dealt with in a variety of ways by my colleagues in the symposium. It is the homunculus crisis: the unitary appearance to a perceiver of perceptual processes that are in fact known to the physiologist to be based upon complex parallel subprocesses.[5] Who or what organizes such a unitary picture: "computations," "algorithms," "invariants," or the homunculus, a little man who has in his head yet another homunculus and so on *ad infinitum*? Who is at home? If it is a homunculus, how could he have been constructed during the wiring of the brain by his cousin, whom we may call "the electrician"? We have already seen that such an electrician, if he exists, has constructed some very odd wiring.

Clearly, any satisfactory theory of higher brain function must remove the need for homunculi and electricians at any level and at the same time must account for object definition and generalization from a world whose events and "objects" are not prelabeled by any a priori scheme or top-down order. This sounds less and less like the tasks computers are put to. How can we meet the issue? I propose that the issue is of precisely the same order as that faced by Darwin when he considered the origins of taxonomic order and the origin of species without assuming a *scalum naturae,* divine intervention, or a superhomunculus[6]. To support this contention, I must consider a few of the main ideas of population thinking, discuss some examples, and then propose how extension of this analysis disposes of the dilemmas and crises I have been discussing.

POPULATION THINKING

Before Darwin, thinking about the origin of biological order was under the sway of an idea that has been variously called the great chain of being, the *scalum naturae,* or for short, essentialism.[7] Since Plato, nature had been assumed to consist of classes, or *taxa,* defined by properties from the top down, fixed and in plenitude. In this view, individual variation was a noisy inconvenience to be ignored, or it was assumed to be a symptom of the fallibility of our earthly life. In any case, the origin of species was assumed by definition.

In creating population thinking, Darwin's great contribution was to make clear that individuality was of the essence, that variance in a population was real and not just noise. Indeed, such variance was the basis for change. Upon this basis, natural selection acted through the environment to select those individuals whose adaptations were on the average "better," that is, eventually leading to their higher rate of reproduction.

Briefly put, these are the basic notions of population thinking, and they provide the main underpinnings for the central theory in biology. All of Darwin's presuppositions, except for his genetics, were correct. Variation within the population is not informed as to outcome; it is by chance. The environment is remorselessly independent, and on the average, the best adapted will survive. It is not a pleasant thought for certain benefactors of modern science that the less fit must eventually die. Nonetheless, these are the basic premises of the theory of natural selection.

I want to turn from the consideration of this global, all-encompassing theory of biology to a very specific example, the immune system. Though the evolutionary system works over aeons of time, this example will show that selective systems can operate in somatic time, that is, within an organism during its lifetime.

The immune system is a system in your body represented by molecules and cells in your blood capable of telling the difference between self and not-self at the molecular level. It is clearly a noncognitive system, despite the attempts of certain Russian biologists to prove that is fundamentally influenced by the brain; nevertheless, it is a system of exquisite specificity. To give you a feeling for that specificity, the immune system can recognize in two huge, otherwise identical protein molecules, the difference of one carbon chain tilted differently in each by just a few degrees. Moreover, it can tell these molecules apart from all other things and retain the ability to do so once it has initially been developed.

Now how can that be? Given all the different compounds that organic chemists can construct that certainly never existed before in the evolution of the human species, how can it be that your body can positively distinguish them and thus distinguish self from not-self in this refined fashion? The theory that prevailed before our most recent modern knowledge was called the theory of instruction. It assumed that, in the immune system, a foreign molecule transferred information about its structure to a cavity in the antibody molecule, the recognizing molecule, and then removed itself much as you might make a cookie with a cookie cutter. That folded crevice would represent an informed recognizing site, which could then recognize all further instances of the particular foreign molecule. You can see why this was called the theory of instruction: information was transferred about three-dimensional structure from the molecule to be recognized to that molecule that would recognize it. That theory has been displaced, but this is not the occasion for me to say how and why. Instead, it will be more to the point to consider the theory that now prevails, the theory of clonal selection.[8]

At first encounter, the idea behind this theory is quite at odds with common sense. It says that *prior* to confrontation with any foreign molecule, your body has the capability of making a huge repertoire of different antibody molecules, each with a different shape at its binding site.[9] When a foreign molecule is introduced into the body, it polls a group of cells (lymphocytes), each with a different kind of antibody on its surface. When it binds to one of sufficiently close complementary shape, it stimulates that cell to divide and make progeny cells bearing more of that kind of antibody with that same complementary shape. This group of daughter cells is a clone, the asexual progeny of a single cell, and this is a case of differential reproduction by clonal selection.

Now, with a little thought one can see some very interesting properties of such a system. In the first place, there is more than one way of recognizing a particular shape above any given threshold criterion for matching shape. In the second place, the system has the potential for memory. Consider, for example, that after presentation of the foreign molecule to a particular group of cells, some cells stop dividing but the rest go on to the end producing antibodies of the kind that would recognize the original foreign molecule. Because some have divided, but not all the way to the end, they constitute a larger number of identical individuals, than was originally present, each waiting to respond to the foreign molecule. Because there are more of them, they can respond more quickly and extensively upon a subsequent presentation of that molecule. This constitutes a form of cellular memory that can last for an entire lifetime.

This argument converges upon two key statements: (1) Essentialism and typological thinking is incorrect; instead, taxa are formed from the bottom up by natural selection.[10] (2) In the immune system in somatic time, instructionism is wrong; instead, recognition of not-self occurs by clonal selection.[11] In both cases, a form of classification upon novelty occurs, an adaptation so refined that in each case the initial idea used to explain it was instructionistic—whether creation by design or transfer of information on foreign molecules to antibodies as they are built.

Now we come full circle to the question about the brain: In its order, does it provide the basis for the recognition of novelty and for generalization by instruction and information processing, or is it, at its most fundamental level of operation, a somatic selective system based upon variance in populations of neurons?[12] To answer this question, I must first discuss a selection theory of brain function and consider the evidence in its favor. This theory should be able to resolve the crises I have described and, in doing so, reconcile the various levels of anatomical, physiological, and psychological function. Otherwise, it would be no improvement over current views.

THE THEORY OF NEURONAL GROUP SELECTION

It is important to point out at the outset that this theory can be described here only in a somewhat skeletal form. This is so because some of its premises touch upon rather detailed and specialized facts concerning nervous systems and their function. Nonetheless, we can state two of the three premises on which it is built in a reasonably simple fashion; the third, we can only gloss in a subsequent section. Those who are interested may consult the original sources for further details.[13]

The theory assumes that during development, groups of neurons are formed in nuclei or laminae of the brain. In any such region, a group numbering from hundreds to thousands of cells represents neurons that are more closely connected to each other than they are to neurons in other groups. The ensemble of all such groups in a region constitutes a repertoire of structural variants—a population. After formation of such groups anatomically during development by means of dynamic processes of cell adhesion that control cell motion and process extension, certain connections are selected over others, and the others disappear.

Once such a primary repertoire is built, a second process of selection occurs during the sojourn of the animal in its environment. The network no longer changes in its geometry. Instead, at any point in time, those groups that respond best to a given input are selected by increasing the efficacy of their synaptic connections. This results in differential amplification of the strengths of certain connections and suppression of others, resulting in the formation of a secondary repertoire. Individuals (groups) in that repertoire will be more likely to respond to similar or identical input signals (or stimuli) than those that were not selected. Nonetheless, although the unit of selection is a group, different groups may compete for neurons, and some neurons in a group may be used to form other groups after competition occurs.

The result of this selection from an already selected anatomical repertoire is the establishment of more than one way of adequately responding to a particular input. This idea that there is, in general, a large number of structurally different groups that may respond in a similar way to a given input or stimulus is called degeneracy. It is a fundamental property of selective systems, and it is the means by which such systems can respond to novel stimuli that are similar but not identical to an original stimulus. It is, in fact, the necessary basis upon which generalizations can be performed by a nervous system.

Degeneracy is not in itself sufficient, however, to support generalization. To understand this point, we must consider the third premise of the theory of neuronal group selection, re-entry, and also take up the issue of categorization of a stimulus world that is not named or ordered a priori. This brings us to the most difficult aspect of the theory, and we must digress a bit to consider how the world of "objects" or "events" that constitute the environment for an animal with a brain might be categorized. After that, we can consider the significance of re-entrant signaling in the brain and its relation to this process of categorization and generalization.

STIMULI, OBJECTS, AND SETS

What is the nature of the stimulus? Is it an essential class—does the world come packaged with labels, as some of the essentialists felt the jungle did for tigers? In other words, is it a list in which singly necessary and jointly sufficient features will define an object —a chair, a table, a leaf, a particular niche, a vein on a leaf, what have you? Or is it, in fact, an arbitrary class, something that the animal simply names for convenience, with no necessary relationship to its other members? You may recognize a kinship in these questions to certain fundamental philosophical questions of realism and nominalism.

Studies on people and on pigeons suggest that neither of these modes reigns.[14] Instead, it appears that a variety of disjunctive features or exemplary properties are used to categorize and generalize. Before describing some of these results, it may be useful to state that real-world stimuli can be grouped into so-called polymorphous sets. These are sets in which disjunctive sampling of features constitutes a class.[15] If a group of things can be characterized by n attributes (where n is not a small number) and any disjunctive combination of m of these features is chosen (where m is less than n), then the ensemble of these combinations constitutes a polymorphous set. If to define a set we insisted upon n

features out of *n*, it would be an essentially defined set, and if we insisted upon only one out of *n* it would be a nominally defined set.

The example shown in figure 2 may serve to make these ideas clearer. The difference between the two groups of patterns is difficult to discern. But when told that members in set I can be characterized by "at least two of round, doubly outlined, or centrally dark," the distinction between the two sets is clear. According to the theoretical position taken here, the world of real stimuli is, in general, polymorphous. But if the world of stimuli is a world of polymorphous sets, the disjunctive properties of which can change depending on the context, the circumstance, or the adaptive needs of the animal, how can an animal use its brain to categorize and generalize in an adaptive manner? Before attempting to answer this question in terms of the theory of neuronal group selection, let me take up some evidence that animals can in fact categorize and generalize without the advantage of language.

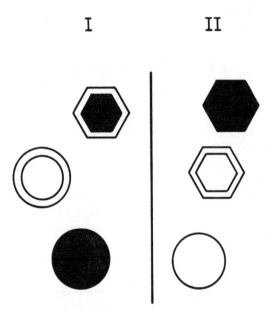

I   II

Figure 2. Polymorphous sets. Set I contains "at least two of round, doubly outlined, or dark." Set II does not. (See note 15.)

OF PIGEONS AND THREE-MONTH-OLD PEOPLE

I will briefly mention two examples of categorization, one by pigeons of visual images and scenes, and one by babies of objects and their boundaries. The pigeon experiments were done by Herrnstein and Cerella. Cerella presented pigeons with images of oak leaves in an operant conditioning mode. After several rewarded presentations, the pigeons positively discriminated oak leaf images from images of all other kinds of leaves.[16] One might surmise that the pigeon's capacity to discriminate these forms was based upon some innate capacity that evolved by natural selection; after all, pigeons and their precursors might have lived among trees, and certain adaptive advantages might have operated on a "hidden cue." But Herrnstein's experiments definitely refute this. He presented pigeons with randomly chosen pictures made by a scuba diver of fish in a variety of contexts. After seeing a small number of these with operant rewards, the pigeons positively discriminated among *novel* pictures, positively picking images of fish.[17]

Pigeons do not live among fish. Moreover, pictures of a particular woman could be used to train a pigeon, after which new images of that particular woman would be positively discriminated in a variety of contexts. One must not assume that the pigeons (which certainly lack language as we know it) are recognizing fish as "fish" or women as "women." Indeed, Cerella has shown that after recognizing images of Charlie Brown (of "Peanuts" fame) and discriminating these from those of Lucy, the pigeons would still recognize Charlie Brown if his head was delineated under his feet. The recognition appears to be largely upon disjunctive collections of local features.

What may we conclude from these findings? I think it is safe to say that the pigeons can generalize without language. In view of the novelty of the images in different contexts, it appears likely that they are recognizing polymorphous sets by particular local features, although this conclusion is less certain. But above all, we can conclude that this behavior cannot be explained by any account of conventional learning. There must exist some additional structural features of pigeon brains that *already* permit such behavior even though reward learning is involved in the original training sets of pictures. No digital computer that we know of can carry out such a general mode of visual pattern recognition without a language and very extensive object descriptions.

Now consider how babies recognize objects. The experiments of E. Spelke suggest that three-month-old babies visually determine object boundaries in two dimensions or in depth by means of the systematic motion of those boundaries relative to occluding objects and a background.[18] A stationary rod occluded by a horizontal one is seen as two separate rods. If this rod is moved horizontally while still occluded, it is seen as a single rod. For our purposes, the most interesting finding is that two separate objects with different colors, textures, and boundary shapes are perceived as one object if they are apposed and made to move together. It seems that a baby (before major language acquisition and the ability to grasp objects definitely) does not "parse" an object by singly necessary and jointly sufficient lists of attributes such as color, shape, and texture, although it may seize upon these to discern the object's motion. For the infant, an "object" is constituted by systematic relative motion of a perceived boundary. This trait does not appear to be learned in any conventional sense but seems, rather, to reflect properties of the infant's visuomotor system. Furthermore, it seems general, that is, it is applied to any moving collection.

With this brief account of these two examples of generalization, we may now turn to the question of how a nervous system could be equipped to carry out such tasks. This requires a return to the theory of neuronal group selection—unfortunately to its most difficult aspect, which is called re-entrant signaling.

RE-ENTRY AND CLASSIFICATION COUPLES

If the world of stimuli consists of potential polymorphous sets sampled by an animal according to its adaptive needs, how can an animal generalize from a small sample? This must reflect an inherent property of the neural networks in its brain. According to the theory of neuronal group selection, that property emerges from three features of the brain (1) re-entrant circuits, (2) the degeneracy of repertoires of neuronal groups, and (3) the arrangement of some of these repertories in maps.

If an object is not predefined or labeled, the nervous system must be able to sample certain of its different features independently and in parallel, for example, through different sensory modalities. In other words, it must be able to sample disjunctively or partition a collection of object features in a variety of independent ways. It must also be able to correlate certain collections of features to constitute entities such as moving boundaries. In this procedure, it must not, however, completely lose cues to the spatiotemporal continuity of an object. Above all, in going from one level of organization of neuronal groups to another in a different part of the brain in short times, it must be able to correlate previous samplings of the same object with current ones, even though the objects do not come labeled, they may move, and they may be occluded.

The requirement for independent sampling is a requirement for a parallel process, and it is well known that the brain is a highly parallel processor. But how, if objects are not labeled, can such a parallel system keep track of them? According to the theory, this is accomplished by re-entrant connections mapping one set of degenerate groups to another (fig. 3). To be concrete, suppose that feature detection (observation of corners, crossings, line stops) could be detected by the visual system. (In fact, we know that such capacities exist inborn and are tuned by experience.) Suppose that, at the same time, the somatosensory system gets signals from the hand moving on the object boundary, correlating the continuity of that boundary. Imagine that neural signals pass independently from each of these sensory systems to separate maps, constituting ordered representations of the visual field or of the body representation for light touch. Now if there *already* exists a mutual set of cross-connections between these two maps that can potentially connect them, we have a re-entrant network.

Groups chosen in one map may be connected by these re-entrant connections to groups independently chosen in the other. Thus, the parallel independent sampling of features on one side and of correlations of features on the other, each chosen disjunctively, are now related to each other. Such an arrangement constitutes the minimal structure capable of independently sampling object attributes for the purpose of classification. This is equiva-

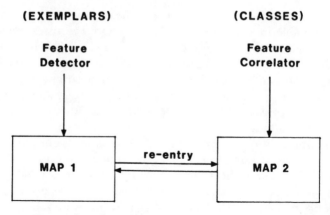

Figure 3. A classification couple using re-entry. Neurons, those in the visual system, for example, act as feature detectors (inheriting that capacity as a result of evolution). They map on the left (map 1) to some higher order lamina in the brain. Other neurons (for example, those related to light touch on a moving finger) act as feature correlators, tracing an object by motion, as shown on the right. These neurons map to another lamina (map 2). The two maps map onto each other by re-entrant connections, so that groups in one map may excite groups in the other. This allows the parallel simultaneous sampling of disjunctive characteristics constituting a polymorphous set in the stimulus; because of the re-entrant connections, these characteristics can be connected in the responses of higher order networks. In this way, certain more general characteristics of an object representation can be connected with other particular characteristics (see note 1).

lent of saying that at least two different modes of sampling must be correlated. In this case, these modes were local visual features and continuity to touch. This smallest unit is called a classification couple. Obviously, in real nervous systems, more than two channels of sampling within or between modalities can be and usually are employed.

Notice that the independent sampling meets the requirement for disjunction—there is no necessary "prelabeled" coupling. Notice also that the arrangement into maps in the nervous system increases the chances of maintaining spatiotemporal continuity in signals that arise from sampling an object. Finally, notice that the function of re-entrant connections between the maps is to help maintain that continuity while linking collections of particular features to other correlations of object properties. This is just what is required to characterize polymorphous sets.

The account I have given here is perforce abstract and may lead you to wonder whether such constructions would actually work. To show that they would in fact do so, my colleague George Reeke, Jr., and I have constructed a new kind of automaton based on these principles.[19] This machine, called Darwin II, is based on the theory of neuronal group selection and is constructed as a classification couple. The world of Darwin II is the stationary collection of all two-dimensional figures in black and white and of a given scale. One side of the couple, called Darwin, consists of an analog of visual feature detection. It is responsible for individual representations: It selects groups giving unique responses to each different stimulus. If a particular collection of features in a stimulus is repeated often, it strengthens the "synapses" or connections of the groups selected so that they are more likely to respond upon subsequent presentations.

The other side of the couple, called Wallace, is responsible for tracing outlines of objects. It yields similar responses or selections of groups when the correlated traces are similar, even for objects that are locally very different, for example, a short, fat letter *A* with a low bar and a rotated, thin, long letter *A* with a high bar.

Re-entry between the higher order networks of Darwin and Wallace gives an interaction between individual and class representations, tying together their independently selected groups. At this point, presentation of an old individual stimulus can call up groups corresponding to other old stimuli by re-entrant linkage (associative memory). Moreover, presentation of novel stimuli of the same class can do the same (generalization).[20]

This is not the place to elaborate on this automaton, which is simulated in very large digital computers as a selective system with 10,000 groups and 10^6 connections. Its performance, which is solipsistic (free of forced learning or programming by its builders) is far from error-free. Indeed, as one might expect, it makes errors about 20 percent of the time. Notice, however, that it deals with novelty within the limits of its construction. Its performance does show the self-consistency of the theory of group selection, but that, of course, has no bearing upon whether the theory is true for real nervous systems. Let me now turn to that subject.

EVIDENCE SUPPORTING THE THEORY

Besides re-entrant circuits and maps, both of which have been amply demonstrated in the brain,[21] the theory of neuronal group selection has two empirical requirements: (1) There must be a generator of diversity during the development of neural circuits, capable of constructing definite patterns of groups but also of generating great individual variation. Variation must occur at the level of cell-to-cell recognition by a molecular process. (2) There must be evidence for group selection and competition in brain maps and re-entrant circuits. This must occur at the level of changes not in the circuitry but in the efficacy of preformed connections or synapses.

Evidence is now accumulating to fulfill each of these requirements. Data to support the first comes from work in our laboratory.[22] For the last decade, we have been studying the molecular mechanism of cell adhesion in the brain and elsewhere. It is adhesion that is responsible for the formation of ensembles of cells and of networks in the brain. We have isolated three kinds of cell adhesion molecules (or CAMs) present at cell surfaces in embryos and responsible for attaching one cell to another. The two from the nervous system are called N-CAM (neural cell adhesion molecule) and Ng-CAM (neuron-glia cell adhesion molecule). A diagram of N-CAM is given in figure 4.

The different molecules have different specificities. N-CAM on one neural cell binds to N-CAM on another. Ng-CAM on the same cell binds to a different molecule on the non-neural support cells of the brain called glia. It is the movement of neurons on glia and of neural processes on each other that gives rise to network patterns in the brain, and the CAMs are intimately involved in assuring this movement and the ensuing pattern. Perturbing the binding of the CAMs leads to disruptions of neural structure.

The key finding for our purposes is this: Neuronal patterns are not assured by preassigned molecular addressing on each cell to construct a "jigsaw puzzle" pattern. Instead, a relatively small number of CAMs on the surfaces of cells switch on and off in sequences defined by their local environment. This dynamic switching changes the patterns of cell motion, of process attachment, and ultimately of the connections formed (see fig. 1).

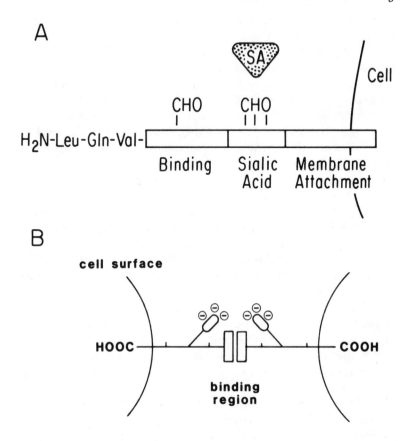

Figure 4. A neural cell adhesion molecule (N-CAM) in diagrammatic form.
A. The molecule consists of three domains, one at the left for binding
another cell (see *B*), a middle domain containing negatively charged sugar
(sialic acid, SA), and a third domain, which is inserted into the cell mem-
brane. *B.* Binding of one N-CAM to another on an apposing cell (homo-
philic binding). H_2N- and COOH refer to the two ends of the polypeptide
or protein chain. The binding of nerve cells to form brain circuits in
embryonic development is controlled by changes in the amount of CAMs
or by chemical changes of N-CAM (reducing the amount of attached sialic
acid). These dynamic changes of the binding in turn control cell movement and axon attachment (see fig. 1) and though they lead to pattern,
they also introduce great variation in the details of the circuity. (See note
22).

Because this so-called cell surface modulation of CAMs on neu-rons depends upon an orderly sequence of environments, it gives a relatively orderly set of circuit patterns. But locally, there is no preassigned exact attachment of a particular neuronal cellular pro-cess to another. We have here a principle, not only of common structure and regulation in the formation of every nervous system, but also of necessary variation. The consequence is that no two nervous systems, even those of twins, can be alike at the level of their fine structure. The necessary variation required by the theory of group selection is supplied by the dynamics of cell surface modulation of CAMs.

This fulfills a necessary but not sufficient condition. Evidence for sufficiency comes from some extraordinary experiments on adult monkeys carried out by Merzenich and his co-workers.[23] These experimenters prepared detailed maps of that portion of the cerebral cortex (the major lamina of the brain) that is con-cerned with the early signals for light touch (fig. 5). They did this by measuring the electrical response of neurons in this area (so-called area 1 and area 3b) as they touched various parts of the monkey's fingers and hand in a systematic fashion. By such a procedure, they could locate the receptive field of a neuron—that part of the skin surface that would make the neuron fire. Working in a systematic fashion, they found continuous regions of cortex corresponding to adjacent receptive fields. These constituted a map of the skin surface of the hand, smooth on the palm and hairy on the back. They then subjected the monkeys to a variety of procedures to see how the maps responded. These procedures consisted of severing one of the three main nerves to the hand, removing one or more digits, and repeatedly stimulating one area, such as the finger pad, by training the monkey to tap its finger for a reward.

The key results of these experiments may be summarized briefly. First, every monkey had a unique map, unlike that of any other monkey. After the median nerve that supplies the smooth skin of the first, second, and half of the third digits was severed, a remarkable change occurred immediately in the map of the owl monkey (fig. 5). A blank area appeared, but more of the dorsal regions of the hand (hairy skin) was represented in areas where it was not previously apparent. Map boundaries changed even for map regions related to the remaining two nerves (radial and ulnar). Then, over a period of months, if the cut median nerve was not allowed to regenerate, the map areas were rearranged in the cortex to correspond to maps assigning territory to either radial

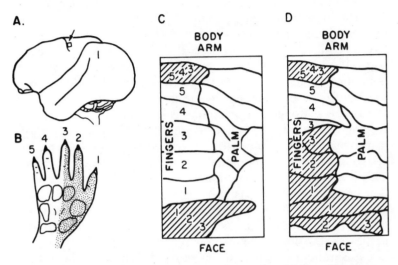

Figure 5. Diagrams illustrating the dynamism and variability of maps serving the sensory modality of light touch in the central cortex of the owl monkey. *A.* A diagram of the brain; the arrow points to the mapped area shown enlarged in *C* and *D*. *B.* A diagram of the palm and digits of the monkey's hand. The shaded portion of the palm is served by the median nerve, the cutting of which causes immediate changes in the normal map (*C*), leading to map *D*. In *C* is shown a map of a normal monkey's cortical area representing the palm and fingers. It is made by stimulating small areas of skin and electrically recording from minute areas around single neurons in the cortex. After severing the median nerve, the map changes, as shown in *D*. The main changes include an increase in the amount of representation of the dorsal skin (shown as diagonally hatched areas in *C* and *D*) and a shift in map boundaries for digits, even those represented by the cortical projections of the two uncut nerves (the radial and ulnar) that also serve the hand. These changes are not due to nerve regrowth. Up to six months later in the adult monkey, the map boundaries continue to shift if the median nerve is not repaired. The diagrams are based on the experiments of Merzenich, et al. (note 23).

or ulnar nerves. There was no evidence that this was because neurons in the mapped regions underwent regrowth and rewiring. Finally, without any surgery at all, it was found that a monkey tapping one finger showed enlargement of the mapped region corresponding to that finger.

The changes seen by these investigators involved continuous movement of map boundaries over considerable distances of cortex. The bulk of the evidence suggests that they are attributable to synaptic changes resulting from alteration in the input. They have been interpreted in terms of the competition for particular cortical cells among neuronal groups that receive overlapping arbors of incoming neurons corresponding to much wider areas of the hand than are apparent in the maps themselves.[24] In other words, the anatomical arrangement is in fact of widespread overlapping arborizations, and, from these overlapping structures, map boundaries are constructed (depending upon the input) by selecting groups through alterations of their synaptic strengths. This is just the picture of competition and selection proposed in the theory of neuronal group selection. Maps are dynamic, they are based on a degenerate repertoire of neuronal groups with variant connections; and it is selection that decides the outcome, in this case the borders of map boundaries. It is extremely difficult to explain these results in terms of fixed, hard-wired neural systems. The results and their analysis indicate that selection is always going on, even in adult brains.[25]

There are a number of other areas in which the theory has received support, for example, in studies of the development of bird song, but the two examples I have given will, I hope, serve to indicate that the theory can explain a number of different, otherwise paradoxical findings. Indeed, each of the issues discussed as crises at the beginning of this chapter actually provides support for the idea of neuronal group selection. I turn briefly to showing how this can be the case.

CRISES RESOLVED

Under this population view of the nervous system, the structural crises precipitated by the absence of precise point-to-point wiring, by the absence of uniquely specific connectivity at the finest ramifications, and by the divergent overlap of dendritic and axonal arbors all dissolve. It is, in fact, just these features of variance one would require to create rich degenerate repertoires for selection. These diverse features are not "noise"; they are necessary variance in neural populations. We have already seen how the regulation of cell interactions by CAMs in embryonic development necessarily leads to both pattern and diversity.

As for the functional crises, silent synapses are not the sign of failure in message transmission. Instead, they are metastable indicators of selection events occurring over the entire population of synapses in a region. As just mentioned, the fluctuations in map borders are signs of neuronal group selection and of successful group competition. The problem of generalization is resolved by re-entrant maps connecting different degenerate repertoires of groups. And finally, multiple parallel processes of re-entry are *required* in order to construct a perceptual response. The apparent coherency and the unitary properties of that response relate to the final process of generalization and memory that emerges from such systems. Lest you think I am disposing of the problem of conscious awareness in a cavalier fashion, I should add that this generalizing property of linked maps with independent inputs structurally constituting a classification couple is only a necessary but not a sufficient property for the awareness of perceptual coherence.

Whatever the ultimate explanation of this awareness, you will perhaps have noticed that in this view of the brain there is no need for a homunculus or for its cousin, the electrician. Just as Darwin's view eliminated the need for creation by design, showing how taxa can be evolved (bottom-up) from populations through natural selection, so this selectionistic view of the brain eliminates the need to create perceptual categories from the top down.

SOME FINAL AND LARGER CONSIDERATIONS

Although the supporting evidence is mounting, I should not leave you with the impression that the theory of neuronal group selection is established. Nonetheless, given the injunction of the organizers of this symposium, it might be valuable to ask what consequences it could have were it proven to be correct. Those consequences are a mixed lot, some scientific, some related to the domain of human values.

The first is that individuality is of the essence in higher brains.[26] In a selective system, the value of a variant cannot be decided a priori: Present judgments of differences in individuals that are based only on past performance are likely to ignore the importance of variance for future change. We can know the value of a variant only after adaptive selection has occurred, and since the future is uncertain, modesty and restraint are in order.

A second consequence is that we must look at all acts of perception as acts of creativity. There is no single way to perceive even when there is apparent agreement at a verbal level. Moreover, in the same vein, memory in such a system is not a replicative recall of stored physical descriptors. It is an imaginative act, a form of dynamic recategorization with decoration by exemplars. Its very lack of repetitive precision in degenerate networks is the source of creative possibility for generalization and pattern recognition.

The larger the size of particular repertoires of neuronal groups, the more adaptive the situation is for conventional learning, which requires prior categorization of a complex world before it can function. According to all these views, no idea can be declared inauthentic a priori by any method, even the scientific method. And a small degree at least of free will and free agency seems to be implicit within such selective systems.

Finally, I come to the main issues of this symposium. The brain is not simply a logic machine; it is not constructed like a digital computer, and if it is a selectional system, as I believe it is, an effective procedure cannot be defined over all its activities a priori.[27] Its fundamental construction is bottom-up through evolution and ontogeny via natural and somatic selection. It is constructed to deal with open-ended situations related to adaptation by generalization in a world that is not locally labeled or named; it is not, in general, rigidly programmed and is not reversible. Sense and survival are its rulers; in humans, logic is only its housekeeper. No one will deny that in such social animals as human beings information processing occurs through social transmission and language. But that evolutionary fact, which has created Larmarckian transmission rules,[28] should not blind us to the essentially Darwinian nature both of the evolution of the brain and of its somatic selectional processes that together govern our fundamental cognitive behavior.

DISCUSSION

Q: *What do you see as the influence of cognitive science on higher education?*

A: First of all, I think it's very easy to forget these days that college education is for fifty years hence, not for tomorrow—something we've learned through history that should stay with us. Regardless of the role of modern technology, libraries remain the one great cultural instrument for recording in some transmissible fashion all forms of human experience: not just scientific and technological knowledge, but values, feelings, and all those other things important to the process of learning.

The first thing to say (and I don't want you to take away the impression that I am diminishing the science that I am so committed to) is that science does have limits. It is not very likely that we can transform a library into a totally scientific instrument any more than we can so transform our lives. That would be to put the origin last. Science comes out of the same human culture and tradition as the arts and the humanities.

The other point I want to make is about brain science. We are really at a very early stage of brain science, and we do not know its limits. My idea of a teacher is a human being—whether he or she uses a computer or not—who is much more interested in the lucid expression of a few ideas than in the vague expression of loads of them. Today's ideas and tomorrow's ideas come and go. I hope that, in the face of technological pressures, we can keep this in mind.

So I would offer the following advice to a young man or woman today: In the first place, master a natural language. Then master one or two computer languages. The term *computer literacy* has a wonderful ring to it, but compared with the rich, ambiguous resources of a natural language, computer languages have not yet reached the level of Keats's *Ode to Psyche* or a play by Shakespeare. Our lives are enriched, in fact, by the ambiguity that gives rise even to scientific ideas.

The task, I think, is to relate this new technology to the past, to preserve a continuity in higher education, and to remember that a college education is for fifty years hence, regardless of economic pressures or technological change.

Q: *(from Daniel Dennett): Professor Edelman, you seem to distinguish rather sharply between two approaches to the study of the brain. One of these you called the information-processing approach; the other, you called the population approach. This puzzled me, because I see a vast range of different approaches. Some of these are preposterously, profoundly unbiological; some are earnestly biological; and some are appropriately neutral on this score. So I didn't see the conflict that you seemed to see between just two approaches. Could you expand a bit on what you meant by the conflict between population thinking and information processing?*

A: First of all, I would like to know a little bit more about what you think is biological, but I'll leave that for later. Perhaps my choice of terms was not the best from a philosophical perspective. What I really meant was something like this: the contrast between essentialism during the development of pre-Darwinian evolutionary theory, as opposed to the theory that Darwin came up with. It has to do with the namer and the name. I agree that the information-processing approach as described, for example, by Professor Schank, is entirely compatible with the biological approach as described, for example, by Dr. Milner—at the level of observable facts. But at the level prior to language, at the level of the confrontation of the organism with its environment, surely you would agree that there is no namer and name in the strict sense.

You would be surprised at how many psychologists I've met —and even neurophysiologists—who actually act as though the world came in nice little packages with category labels on them. They talk about information going down one neuron, stimulating a neurotransmitter, and being transferred to another neuron. But when you actually go looking for this "information," you find instead a whole host of hidden and unexamined assumptions. It is this casual and uncritical use of the term *information processing* that I had in mind.

Q: *If your population model is correct, is it not true that the theory of relativity, all of Shakespeare's works, and indeed all of past, present, and future knowledge is buried within the mind of each of us, and that tapping that knowledge is only a matter of "pressing the correct combination or permutation of buttons"?*

A: This gives me the opportunity to come back to Professor Dennett's question. It is exactly this that is *not* implied by the model, nor is it implied by evolutionary thinking. What is implied by the model is the potential or the capacity, upon interaction with appropriate environments, to *do* all these things—not the existence of precise information, as though someone could say, "Let there be Shakespeare plays," and then the only problem would be to tickle them out.

It was exactly this (incorrect) sort of thinking that accounted for the existence of different species before Darwin. A tiger was a tiger. If someone said, "But this tiger has a long nose and clear spots," the reply would be, "That's just a sport. It's noise. It doesn't matter."

But it is the fundamental point of selectionist models that they do not have information built except *ex post facto.* It is after selection has occurred and adaptations have differentially survived that information is defined—not before. Anything that works will do. It is extremely important to infer from evolutionary theory that there is no progress. There might be increasing complexity, but there is no value judgment about what's better or more fit. If it works, it works. In other words, you don't design a bird's wing using aerodynamics. What you do is extend a leg, if that works. This is an important point to make, because it is commonly confusing to people when they first hear about selectionist models. They think everything is stored away ahead of time as though in a dictionary. That isn't the case. It is the *potential for making a good enough choice* that is built into biological systems.

Q: *How many different compounds are found in the neighborhood of a synapse?*

A: That's a very good question indeed. We say that a neurotransmitter is released when an electrical signal reaches the area where one neuron touches another. In fact, we are discovering an extraordinary number of neurotransmitters. I wouldn't say one every day, but the classes of them are expanding at a fantastic rate.

There are two main classes of neurotransmitters. One is

excitatory and makes the next neuron more likely to fire. The other is inhibitory and decreases the tendency to fire. But there are a whole set of compounds—some of which are the peptide or protein functional analogues of opium and morphine, that is, the endorphins—that act as modulators of the system. So you have several kinds of neurotransmitters, and they differ in function.

People are studying the region in the second neuron that receives the neurotransmitter, the so-called receptor, or channel. Now it is that channel that is changed by binding a neurotransmitter and that makes the next neuron fire. The interesting thing is that such channels are found, not only in neurons, but all the way down in evolution, and the number of them is simply staggering. The one that amuses me the most is the one that makes the paramecium reverse its direction. It's a calcium channel, and when the paramecium bumps into something, the calcium channel changes its conformation, or shape, in such a way as to reverse the direction of the hairs that make the paramecium swim. Evolution is incredible.

The lesson that you take away from examples like this is that the brain, as Dr. Milner would describe it, is in a tight, bony box. After you develop all these billions of connections, the fact is that you can't really grow much more. Then nature comes along with a very clever device: You don't have just one neurotransmitter. You change the grammar by having a whole bunch, and you use the neuronal circuits in different ways by changing the chemistry.

A beautiful example has been found recently in the so-called stomatogastric ganglion of the lobster, of all things. This ganglion controls how the lobster's stomach contracts. It has different neurotransmitters, and, depending on the ratio, the same wiring will do two different things, or three different things, or four. So we find that billions of possibilities are multiplied by countless others.

Q   *(from Daniel Dennett): I'm reminded by your "Darwin II" model of the perceptron, in which each component had adaptive and selective properties. I seem to recall that perceptrons failed to behave intelligently because of an over simple organization. Would you comment, please?*

A: The perceptron was an early, pioneering attempt to develop an automaton that did not have a program but that adapted to certain limited environments. The automaton that we have built differs in a great number of technical details from the perceptron. One of the major differences is that our system is so constituted that it is a selective machine. A perceptron is not. The perceptron simply had a wiring scheme in which a response could be reinforced if it was the right one under the circumstances. The perceptron's perception was very rigid. You couldn't move an object half an inch, or rotate it, without having it perceived as a different object. Our system takes account of these variations by a set of mechanisms that I won't describe in detail here. But it performs quite differently from the perceptron.

NOTES

1. G. M. Edelman, "Group Selection and Phasic Reentrant Signaling: A Theory of Higher Brain Function, in *The Mindful Brain,* ed. G. M. Edelman and V. Mountcastle (Cambridge, Mass.: MIT Press, 1978), pp. 51–100; "Group Selection as the Basis for Higher Brain Function, in *The Organization of the Cerebral Cortex: Proceedings of a Neurosciences Research Program Colloquium,* ed. F. O. Schmitt, et al. (Cambridge, Mass.: MIT Press, 1981), pp. 535–63. G. M. Edelman and G. N. Reeke, Jr., "Selective Networks Capable of Representative Transformation, Limited Generalizations, and Associative Memory, *Proc. Natl. Acad. Sci. USA* 79:2091–2095 (1982). G. M. Edelman and L. H. Finkel, "Neuronal Group Selection in the Cerebral Cortex," in *Dynamic Aspects of Neocortical Function,* ed. G. M. Edelman, W. E. Gall, and W. M. Cowan (New York: John Wiley & Sons, 1984), pp. 653–95. L. H. Finkel and G. M. Edelman, "Interaction of Synaptic Modification Rules Within Populations of Neurons, *Proc. Natl. Acad. Sci. USA,* in press.
2. For a general introductory review, see G. M. Shepherd, *Neurobiology,* (New York: Oxford University Press, 1983).
3. D. Purves and J. W. Lichtman, *Principles of Neural Development,* (Sunderland, Mass.: Sinauer Associates, 1985).
4. Edelman and Finkel, "Neuronal Group Selection in the Cerebral Cortex."
5. G. M. Edelman, "Through a Computer Darkly: Group Selection and Higher Brain Function, Stated Meeting Report for the American Academy of Arts and Sciences, Boston, 1981, *Bulletin of the American Academy of Arts and Sciences* 36:18–49 (1982).
6. E. Mayr, *The Growth of Biological Thought: Diversity, Evolution, and Inheritance,* (Cambridge, Mass.: Belknap Press of Harvard University Press, 1982).
7. Ibid.
8. F. M. Burnet, *The Clonal Selection Theory of Acquired Immunity,* (Nashville, Tenn.: Vanderbilt University Press, 1959).
9. G. M. Edelman, "Antibody Structure and Molecular Immunology, *Science* 180: 830–840 (1973).

10. Mayr, *Growth of Biological Thought.*
11. Burnet, *Clonal Selection Theory of Acquired Immunity;* Edelman, "Antibody Structure and Molecular Immunology."
12. Edelman, "Group Selection and Phasic Reentrant Signaling"; "Group Selection as the Basis for Higher Brain Function"; "Through a Computer Darkly."
13. Edelman, "Group Selection and Phasic Reentrant Signaling"; Finkel and Edelman, "Interaction of Synaptic Modification Rules"; Edelman, "Through a Computer Darkly."
14. E. E. Smith and D. L. Medin, *Categories and Concepts,* Harvard (Cambridge, Mass.: Harvard University Press, 1981). J. Cerella, "Visual Classes and Natural Categories in the Pigeon, *J. Exp. Psy.: Hum. Percept. Perform.* 5:68–77 (1979). R. J. Herrnstein, "Stimuli and the Texture of Experience," *Neurosci. and Biobehavioral Rev.* 6:105–117 (1982).
15. I. Dennis, J. A. Hampton, and S. E. G. Lea, "New Problem in Concept Formation," *Nature* 243:101–102 (1973).
16. Cerella, "Visual Classes and Natural Categories in the Pigeon."
17. Herrnstein, "Stimuli and the Texture of Experience."
18. T. J. Kellman and E. S. Spelke, "Perception of Partly Occluded Objects in Infancy, *Cognitive Psych.* 15:483–524 (1983).
19. Edelman and Reeke, "Selective Networks Capable of Representative Transformation, Limited Generalizations, and Associative Memory."
20. Ibid.; G. N. Reeke, Jr., and G. M. Edelman, "Selective Networks and Recognition Automata" *Ann. N. Y. Acad. Sci.,* in press.
21. Edelman and Finkel, "Neuronal Group Selection in the Cerebral Cortex"; Shepherd, *Neurobiology.*
22. G. M. Edelman, "Cell Adhesion Molecules: A Molecular Basis for Animal Form", *Scientific American* 250:118–129 (1984); G. M. Edelman, "Modulation of Cell Adhesion During Induction, Histogenesis, and Perinatal Development of the Nervous System", *Ann. Rev. Neurosci.* 7:339–377 (1984).
23. M. M. Merzenich, J. H. Kaas, J. T. Wall, R. J. Nelson, M. Sur, and D. J. Fellerman, "Topographic Reorganization of Somatosensory Cortical Areas 3b and 1 in Adult Monkeys Following Restricted Deafferentation", *Neurosci.* 8:33–55 (1983); "Progression of Change Following Median Nerve Section in the Cortical Representation of the Hand in Areas 3b and 1 in Adult Owl and Squirrel Monkeys", *Neurosci.* 10:639–665 (1983).
24. Edelman and Finkel, "Neuronal Group Selection in The Cerebral Cortex."
25. Ibid.
26. Edelman, "Through a Computer Darkly."
27. Ibid.
28. P. J. Richerson and R. Boyd, "A Dual Inheritance Model of the Human Evolutionary Process I: Basic Postulates and a Simple Model", *J. Social Biol. Struct.* 1:127–154 (1978).

2. Memory and the Human Brain

BRENDA MILNER

The invitation to take part in the Nobel Conference gave me particular pleasure, because I still have vivid memories of an earlier visit to Gustavus, a few years ago, and it is owing to such memory processes that today I know something of this college, and by the time I leave, this knowledge will have been enriched and brought up to date. In this sense, the question of "How We Know" is seen to be closely linked to the narrower question of "How We Remember." It is the latter topic that I have chosen to address, by describing the differing effects on memory of various circumscribed lesions of the human brain, and by considering the implications of these findings for our understanding of how memory is organized in the intact nervous system. This work with patients extends back over thirty years, but my own interest in memory goes back even further, to my undergraduate days at Cambridge, as a student in Bartlett's laboratory. I was therefore delighted to hear Dr. Edelman say that memory is selective, rather than a passive reproduction of external events. This was Bartlett's main message, and, although it is not a notion on which I shall be elaborating here, it is implicit in all that follows.

The chapter has three parts: First, I describe the main features of the global amnesic syndrome that follows extensive bilateral damage to structures deep under the surface of the brain, on the medial aspect of the temporal lobes. This material may be familiar through the much-publicized patient HM, but it is crucial to the argument I wish to develop here. Secondly, I discuss the milder, specific memory deficits that are observed in patients who have undergone a unilateral anterior temporal lobectomy for the relief

This work was supported by the Medical Research Council of Canada.

of long-standing epilepsy. Lastly, I shall present evidence for a contribution from the frontal lobes to the temporal organization and segregation of events in memory.

At the outset, I should like to reflect briefly on the kind of memory that we take for granted, such as being able to recall listening to a lecture we have just heard or eating lunch or what the weather is outside when we are inside. What is remarkable about this ability is that in the interim we have turned our attention to other matters, yet without any special effort we can still recall such events from the recent past and can recognize again people, objects, and situations we have recently encountered for the first time. As we shall see, it is this kind of memory that is selectively impaired in the amnesic syndrome, leaving other cognitive processes and many other learning skills intact.

MEMORY LOSS AFTER BILATERAL MEDIAL
TEMPORAL-LOBE RESECTION: CASE HM

Our most detailed knowledge of the memory disorder resulting from bilateral damage to the medial structures of the temporal lobes comes from the study of a young man, HM, in whom Dr. William B. Scoville of Hartford, Connecticut, had carried out a bilateral medial temporal-lobe resection for the relief of epilepsy; however, other patients with similarly situated lesions of both cerebral hemispheres have shown the same pattern of memory loss.[1]

HM was an assembly line worker by trade, but since the age of 16 he had been subject to major epileptic seizures that had increased in frequency and severity despite heavy anticonvulsant medications, so that by the age of 27 he was no longer able to work or lead a normal life. On August 23, 1953, in hope of alleviating this condition, Dr. Scoville performed the brain operation illustrated in Figure 1. The removals extended back along the medial surface of each hemisphere for a distance of about eight centimeters, destroying the uncus and amygdala on both sides, together with the anterior two-thirds of the hippocampus and parahippocampal gyrus, but sparing the temporal neocortex.

Already in the first few postoperative days it was apparent that HM had a grave memory impairment. Thus, it was noted that he could no longer recognize the hospital staff (except Dr. Scoville,

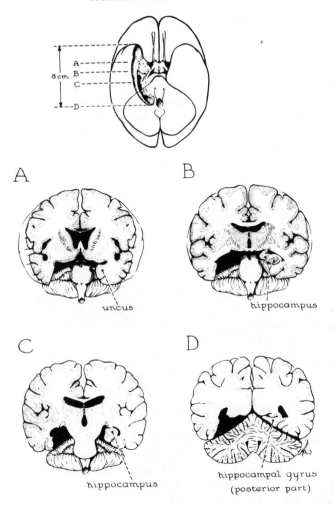

Figure 1. Diagrammatic cross sections of the human brain, illustrating the reported extent of bilateral medial temporal-lobe resection in patient HM. At the top is a drawing of the base of the brain, showing where the various cross sections have been taken. The amygdala would have appeared in a section between *A* and *B* but is not shown here. Note that, for demonstration purposes, the excision is shown on the right side of the brain only and the corresponding intact structures on the left. (*Reproduced by permission of the American Psychiatric Association*).

whom he had known for many years); nor could he remember or relearn the way to the bathroom or recall anything of the day-to-day happenings in the hospital. He also showed a patchy retrograde amnesia for events of the past three years, including the death of a favorite uncle. His earlier memories appeared to be intact; his speech was normal; and his social behavior was entirely appropriate. Except for some reduction in the length of the retrograde amnesia, this condition has persisted essentially unchanged to the present day.

Because medial temporal-lobe resections limited to the uncus and amygdala do not cause generalized memory loss, it is sometimes assumed that the hippocampal lesions were alone responsible for the memory deficits seen in HM. It is therefore worth noting that Mishkin has recently demonstrated a loss of recognition memory in monkeys following bilateral removal of amygdala and hippocampus, with no deficit of comparable magnitude following removal of either structure alone. It thus seems possible that some aspects of HM's memory impairment may represent the combined effects of the two lesions, with consequent disruption of two functionally equivalent neural circuits.[2]

Since undergoing this radical brain operation, HM has had few major seizures, and, perhaps for this reason, his concentration has improved and his IQ has risen from 104 to 117. In 1955, when I first began to work with him, it was clear that forgetting occurred the instant the focus of his attention shifted, but that in the absence of distraction his capacity for sustained attention was remarkable. Thus, he was able to retain the number 584 for over fifteen minutes by continuously rehearsing an elaborate mnemonic scheme. When asked how he had been able to remember the number for so long, he replied, "It's easy. You just remember 8. You see, 5, 8, and 4 add to 17. You remember 8, subtract it from 17, and it leaves 9. Divide 9 in half and you get 5 and 4, and there you are: 584. Easy." A minute later, he was unable to recall either the number 584 or any of the associated complex train of thought; in fact, he no longer knew that he had been given a number to remember, because in the meantime the examiner had introduced a new topic.

This discontinuity between the maintenance of an item in an active memory system for fifteen minutes and the loss of the whole episode after an interruption supports the distinction between primary and secondary memory made long ago by William James.[3] According to James, "An object of primary memory is not . . . brought back [into consciousness]," because "it was never lost." In contrast:

Memory proper, or secondary memory, . . . is the knowledge of a former stage of mind after it has already dropped from consciousness; or rather, the knowledge of an event, or fact, of which meantime we have not been thinking.

The nervous system appears to respect this distinction, primary memory being spared in HM and secondary memory, insofar as it applies to postoperative events, being severely impaired.

HM's failure to retain new information after a single presentation does not rule out the possibility that he might be able to acquire some new knowledge after many repetitions of a situation, or even that certain kinds of learning might proceed at a normal rate. Accordingly, in 1960, seven years after the operation, I attempted to train him on two different learning tasks, with widely divergent results.

The first task was to learn the route through the stylus maze shown in Figure 2. Here the circles represent metal boltheads that provide visible "stepping-stones," and the black line indicates the correct path, which is, of course, invisible to the subject. Every time the subject's metal stylus touches a bolthead that is not on the correct path, an error-counter clicks noisily, informing him of his mistake. He thus proceeds by trial and error, with the counter as his guide.

This task is not difficult for normal subjects, who usually achieve errorless performance within 20 trials. HM failed to show any learning at all after 215 trials spread over three days, and at the end he was still having "a little argument" with himself over which way to turn at the first choice-point. In retrospect, this failure is less surprising than it seemed at the time. This maze has twenty-eight choice-points, so that, even with recourse to verbal mnemonics, it is hard to see how HM could have encompassed the entire sequence of turns within the span of immediate memory. He would thus inevitably have forgotten the first part of the route by the time he reached the end. In an attempt to resolve this problem,

MAZE

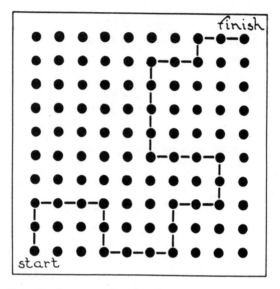

Figure 2. Plan of stylus maze, showing the route to be learned. The circles represent metal boltheads on a black wooden base. *(Reproduced by permission of the Centre National de la Recherche Scientifique, Paris).*

I later gave him intensive training on a shortened form of the maze that contained only six choice-points and thus did not exceed his memory span. Even under these conditions, HM's learning was extraordinarily slow, requiring 155 trials before he attained the criterion of three successive errorless runs.

These experimental findings parallel the slow learning of spatial relationships manifested by HM in everyday life. Shortly after the operation, his family moved to a new house a few blocks from where they had formerly lived. It seems to have taken him about five years to learn the spatial layout of the new house and to remember where objects in constant use (such as the lawn mower) were kept. However, once acquired, this knowledge was retained, and he was even able to draw an accurate floor plan of this house after he had ceased to live there. We do not know how such cognitive maps are represented in the brain, but presumably they involve large populations of cells widely distributed within specialized regions of the cerebral cortex. What is impressive is to realize how slowly they are established when the normal medial temporal-lobe input to the cortex is absent.

The second task on which HM was trained in 1960 involved the acquisition of a visuomotor skill, and enabled me to demonstrate that not all forms of learning are impaired in amnesia. The task, mirror drawing, required the subject to draw a line that followed the circumference of a five-pointed star and stayed within its narrow border (see Figure 3), the subject being unable to observe either his hand or the star directly but only as reflected in a mirror. This task is difficult at first, but normal subjects rapidly improve with practice. Figure 4 shows that the same was true for HM; he had a normal learning curve over the three-day training period, beginning each new session at the level he had attained at the end of the previous day. On the other hand, he remained totally unaware that he had done the task before; this was learning without any sense of familiarity.[4].

HM's success on the mirror-drawing task led me to speculate that other kinds of motor skill might also be acquired independently of the medial temporal-lobe system. By this, I had in mind such activities as learning to dance or swim or to pronounce a foreign language (though not, of course, to master its syntax or vocabulary). Such skills are built up gradually without our being able to describe just what it is that we are learning, and the attempt to introspect is likely to impair performance. It seemed reasonable to suppose that such kinds of learning would not require the participation of a conscious, cognitive memory system.

This generalization has held up whenever it has been tested, although the skills sampled so far have been few and of limited complexity. It is now clear, however, that the original formulation was too narrow, and that it is not only motor skills but also various other kinds of learning that are preserved in amnesia. Thus, Warrington and Weiskrantz found that amnesic patients could learn to identify fragmented drawings of objects and animals with progressively fewer cues, even though they did not remember having seen the drawings before,[5] a finding that I subsequently replicated with HM. The task was a modified version of the Incomplete Figures Test devised by Gollin for use with children. The stimuli consisted

MIRROR DRAWING TASK

Figure 3. Star pattern used in the mirror-drawing task. Starting from S, the subject has to trace the outline with a pencil, keeping within the lines. Crossing a line constitutes an error. (*Reproduced by permission of the Centre National de la Recherche Scientifique, Paris*).

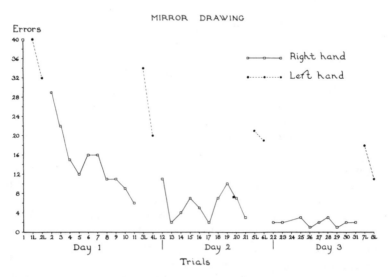

Figure 4. Mirror-drawing performance of HM, showing normal learning over the three-day period. (*Reproduced by permission of the Centre National de la Recherche Scientifique, Paris*).

of twenty realistic line drawings, each of which could be presented in a series graded in difficulty from 1 (the most sketchy outline) to 5 (the complete, easily identifiable picture). Figure 5 shows a typical item: a sketchy, fragmented drawing of an airplane, the outline of which becomes progressively better delineated from its first presentation in Set 1 to its final presentation in Set 5.

Subjects are shown the most fragmented drawings first (Set 1) and are encouraged to guess promptly what each drawing might be. This procedure is then repeated through progressively easier sets, until all twenty drawings have been correctly identified. Failure to name, or misnaming, constitutes an error.

On first encounter with this task, HM made fewer errors than the mean for the normal control group, a finding that is consistent with his good performance on many other perceptual tasks. On retesting, one hour later, HM did not show as much improvement as the control group, who had the advantage of being able to remember the names of the objects they had been shown before and therefore knew what to expect. Nevertheless, he reduced his error score by 48 percent, with residual learning still evident on further testing, four months later. At this point we should bear in mind that the drawings when complete could be named instantly by a young child. Hence, when HM learned to identify them with fewer contour cues, he was exhibiting a lowered threshold for

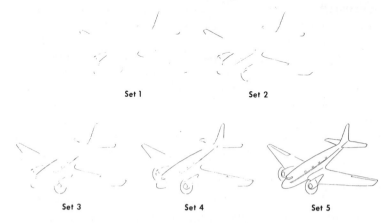

Figure 5. Sample item from the incomplete-figures task. (*Reproduced by permission of Pergamon Press, Oxford*).

activation of well-established representations in the brain, rather than the acquisition of new information.[6] Difficult as it is to imagine how such long-term "priming" effects are mediated, the underlying processes are clearly dissociable from those involved in the recall and recognition of past events.

And so the instances of spared learning multiply, and no doubt will continue to do so, as more and more learning tasks are given to amnesic patients. Of particular interest has been the demonstration by Cohen[7] that amnesic subjects (including HM) can with practice learn to solve the Tower of Hanoi problem, mentioned by Dr. Simon in Chapter 4. The task requires the subject to transfer a set of slotted discs from the first to the third of three vertical rods without ever placing a larger disc on top of a smaller one. HM succeeded eventually in doing this in the minimum number of moves, and, as usual, without realizing that he had done the task before. This and related evidence that not only sensorimotor but also some cognitive skills can be acquired by amnesic patients led Cohen and Squire to characterize what is spared in amnesia as "procedural" learning (learning how to do something); the ability to acquire "declarative" knowledge (knowing what) is lost. Although this is perhaps as good a dichotomy as any, I am not sure that it is wise to try to subsume all spared learning abilities under one heading, since many different kinds of learning may be going on in parallel, and, at least in the case of HM, it seems that just the conscious cognitive memory system is no longer functioning.

Up to this point in my analysis of HM's memory impairment I have been ignoring the important distinction made by Endel Tulving[8] between episodic and semantic memory, both of which, I shall argue, are disturbed in amnesia. Episodic memory, as the name implies, refers to the personal, autobiographical kind of memory, with its temporal reference to past events, whereas semantic memory is exemplified in our acquired cognitive structure of the meanings of words and in the broad framework of our conceptual knowledge. Though few would deny that the most salient feature of any amnesic syndrome is the loss of episodic memory (as here defined), the status of semantic memory in amnesia has been a matter for debate. For instance, it has been suggested that, because HM's preoperatively acquired semantic knowledge was unaffected by the radical medial temporal-lobe resection, therefore his semantic memory system is spared. To me, this begs the whole question of how semantic knowledge is built up in the first place, and the related, more specific question of how much new knowledge HM has in fact been able to acquire over the many years that have elapsed since the operation.

Recently, John Gabrieli, in Dr. Suzanne Corkin's laboratory at MIT, has begun to explore this question, taking advantage of the fact that Webster's dictionary is updated every five years by the inclusion of words that have become current in the language since the previous edition was compiled. Gabrieli has used a variety of experimental techniques to assess HM's knowledge of such words, and has shown that he has learned far fewer new words than a control group of the same age. Along similar lines, a former student of mine, Mary Lou Smith, has been exploring HM's notions of what such common objects as cars, clocks, radios, and washing machines look like these days, and has found that his representations of these objects have not kept up with the times. Lest this ignorance be attributed to the sheltered life that HM leads, it should be pointed out that he watches television assiduously and is exposed to advertisements in magazines. HM's factual knowledge has, in fact, expanded with constant exposure to television, so that, for example, he now has some idea of astronauts and space travel, but such knowledge is meager and unreliable.

Preliminary as these investigations are, I believe that they support the idea that the medial temporal-lobe structures play a role in the acquisition of semantic as well as episodic knowledge, and that in their absence such knowledge can only be acquired slowly, over many repetitions.

MEMORY AND HEMISPHERIC SPECIALIZATION: CONTRASTING EFFECTS OF LEFT AND RIGHT TEMPORAL-LOBE LESIONS

It is because HM's operation was bilateral, depriving him of the functions of amygdala and hippocampus on both sides of the brain, that he suffered such a severe and generalized memory loss. By contrast, the operation of unilateral anterior temporal lobectomy is a well-recognized treatment for temporal-lobe epilepsy and can be carried out safely without risk of global amnesia, provided the medial temporal-lobe structures of the opposite hemisphere are functioning normally. In such cases, one does see certain specific memory deficits, which vary with the side of the epileptogenic lesion and reflect the complementary specialization of the two cerebral hemispheres. Thus, injury to the left temporal lobe, in the hemisphere dominant for speech, impairs memory for verbal information, irrespective of the sensory channel. Whether listening to a lecture or reading a book, patients with such lesions complain that they cannot recall as well as they should the material that they have been studying. A corresponding injury to the opposite, right temporal lobe, is not associated with verbal memory difficulty but rather with complementary deficits affecting the recall and recognition of visual and auditory patterns (such as faces or melodies), which cannot readily be coded in words.

These deficits can often be detected preoperatively, reflecting the presence of abnormally functioning tissue in one temporal lobe, but after operation the deficits tend to be exacerbated, even though the general level of intellectual functioning may improve. We have also found that the appearance of postoperative impairments on certain tasks depends on whether or not the hippocampus and parahippocampal gyrus have been included in the removal. These are findings that I should like to illustrate here, beginning with an experiment showing the contribution of the left hippocampal region to verbal recall and going on to consider the role of the right hippocampal region in spatial memory.

All the data to be reported derive from the study of patients who are left-hemisphere dominant for speech. This means that propositional speech and writing are mediated solely by that hemisphere, although, as Sperry and his associates have shown, the right hemisphere is capable of some rudimentary comprehension of language.

VERBAL MEMORY AND THE LEFT TEMPORAL LOBE

Figure 6 depicts the approximate location of critical areas in the inferior frontal and posterior temporo-parietal regions of the left hemisphere where brief electrical stimulation of the exposed cortex during surgery may momentarily interfere with speech,[9] and where injury in adult life is apt to cause lasting language impairment. In the neurosurgical treatment of epilepsy, great care is

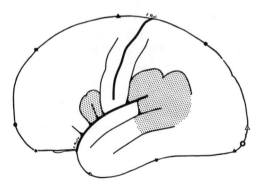

Figure 6. Diagram showing the lateral surface of the left cerebral hemisphere. Stippling indicates location of the speech areas. (*Reproduced by permission of Springer-Verlag, Berlin*).

taken that the removal should not encroach upon these primary speech areas, but extensive cortical excisions can be made outside these areas without risk to language.

In the operation of unilateral temporal lobectomy, the removal always includes the anterior temporal neocortex and the amygdala, damage to the latter structure being most frequently responsible for the patient's epilepsy. In some cases, however, it is also necessary to excise part of the hippocampus and overlying parahippocampal gyrus if the patient's seizures are to be controlled. In order to determine whether adding the hippocampal removal leads to any specific changes in memory, we now routinely subdivide our subjects with temporal lobe lesions not only according to side of operation but, also with respect to the extent of hippocampal excision. This classification results in four temporal-lobe groups: a left temporal-lobe group (LTh) with small, and one (LTH) with large, excisions from the hippocampal area and, likewise, a right temporal-lobe group (RTh) with little, and one (RTH) with extensive, damage to the hippocampal region. Figure 7 shows a typical removal in each of the four groups.

In analyzing the effects of left or right temporal lobectomy, it is important to keep in mind that the operations differ from HM's not only in being unilateral but also in involving the anterior temporal neocortex. We may therefore expect to see some postoperative deficits that reflect the specializations of that area and not merely the contributions of amygdala and hippocampus. This is apparent in the results of the verbal memory experiment by Donald Read.

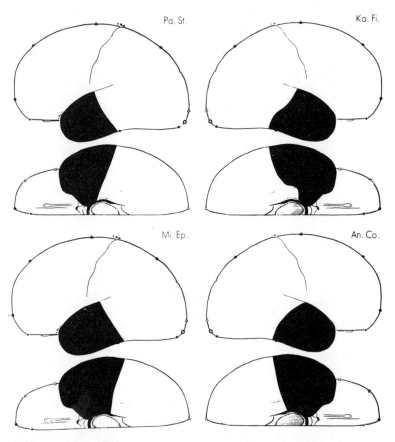

Figure 7. Brain maps based on the surgeon's drawings, at the time of operation, showing (in black) the estimated extent of removal in representative left and right temporal lobectomies (lateral surface above, inferior surface below). Case Pa. St., left temporal, small hippocampal removal (LTh); Case Mi. Ep., left temporal, large hippocampal removal (LTH); Case Ka. Fi., right temporal, small hippocampal removal (RTh); Case An. Co., right temporal, large hippocampal removal (RTH).

This experiment had its origin in the well-established finding that, when we try to recall a long list of words, in any order, after a single exposure to them, we show better recall for the first words of the list (primacy effect) and the last words of the list (recency effect) than we do for those in the middle.[10] These serial order effects bring us back to the distinction between primary and secondary memory. Thus, the last, or most recent, words on the list have an advantage in recall because they are still in primary memory, whereas the earlier items have to be retrieved from secondary memory. In this case, the words at the beginning of the list would be favored over those in the middle, because they would be subject to less interference from preceding items and might also have benefited from more mental rehearsal. With these interpretations in mind, Read set out to study the effects of unilateral temporal lobectomy on the recall of word lists. Because patients with left temporal-lobe lesions do poorly on most verbal memory tasks, Read expected both the LTh and LTH groups to recall fewer words overall than the right temporal-lobe groups, who should perform normally. Of more theoretical interest was his prediction that the LTH group in particular would show a reduced primacy effect, on the hypothesis that the left hippocampal region plays a significant role in facilitating the retention of words in secondary memory.

It has been shown that subjects remember words better that they have themselves generated according to some rule, rather than words to which they have listened passively. For this reason, Read used a word-generation technique[1] to study list recall. The technique has the further advantage of ensuring that attention is paid to every word on the list. Subjects were required to generate two lists of sixteen words each, one on the basis of sound (rhymes) and the other on the basis of meaning (synonyms). For the rhymes, the target words were produced in response to clues of the form: "A word that rhymes with rice and begins with N." For the synonyms, a typical clue would be: "A word that means big and begins with L." The rhymes and the synonyms were given on different days, in a balanced design, and in each case the subjects were tested for recall of the sixteen target words immediately after completion of the list, as well as one hour later.

On both these verbal recall tasks, patients with right temporal-lobe lesions performed normally, with no differences between the RTh and RTH groups. As predicted, the left temporal-lobe groups exhibited impairments, but with the pattern of results for the rhymes task differing from that obtained for the synonyms. This difference is quite striking when immediate recall scores are plotted as a function of the position of the words in the list.

Figure 8 shows the serial position curves for the normal control group and the two left temporal-lobe groups for the immediate recall of the list of words generated as rhymes. The curve for the control group illustrates the expected primacy and recency effects, subjects recalling more words from the beginning and end of the list than from the middle, whereas both left temporal-lobe groups show only a recency effect. The fact that the LTh group, in whom the hippocampus had been largely or entirely spared, still showed such extremely poor recall from secondary memory for words generated on the basis of their sounds suggests that the left anterior temporal cortex plays a special role in the evocation of the sounds of words, a conclusion for which there is already considerable support from other studies in these patients.

Figure 9 shows the serial position curves of the same three groups for the immediate recall of words generated according to

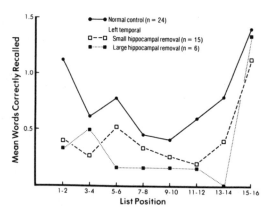

Figure 8. Recall of word lists (rhymes): serial position curves obtained by Read for the immediate recall of words generated as rhymes, showing loss of primacy effect after left temporal lobectomy, irrespective of extent of hippocampal removal.

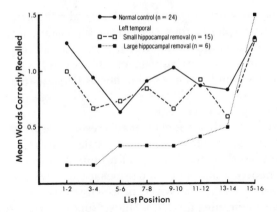

Figure 9. Recall of word lists (synonyms): serial position curves for immediate recall of words generated as synonyms, showing loss of primacy effect to be contingent upon radical excision from the hippocampal region.

their meaning. Words that are processed semantically are normally recalled better than words processed phonetically,[12] and hence a somewhat higher overall level of recall was to be expected. This is seen in the results of the normal control group, together with the usual recency and primacy effects. In addition, one notes a striking difference between the results of the two left temporal-lobe groups. Again both groups show a normal recency effect, but this time Group LTh, with the hippocampus spared, shows also a normal primacy effect, recalling as many words from the beginning of the list as the control group, whereas Group LTH, with the hippocampus excised, has no primacy effect at all, recalling virtually no words from the beginning of the list. Thus, these results provide direct evidence that the left hippocampal region can play a critical role in the retention of words beyond the stage of primary memory.

To understand why different findings were obtained on these two tasks, it is important not to think of the hippocampus as related only to the temporal lobe, even though it happens to be situated on the inner surface of that lobe. Recent anatomical studies[13] have demonstrated rich reciprocal connections that link the hippocampal region (by which I mean the hippocampus and overlying parahippocampal gyrus) to widespread neocortical areas of the same hemisphere, thus permitting a constant interplay between the hippocampus and different cortical areas involved in the encoding and long-term storage of information. On this view, then, memory could be impaired either by damage to a particular neocortical area or by interference with the connections of that area to the hippocampal region.

If we now apply this model to Read's results, we see that the left temporal neocortex played an essential role in the re-evocation of the rhymes, so that the addition of a hippocampal lesion to the temporal neocortical removal did not exacerbate the memory loss. On the synonyms task, however, in which words are encoded according to their meaning, one must suppose that the words achieve a much wider representation in the left hemisphere, so that the memory survives removal of the anterior temporal cortex, at least for immediate recall (although a slight loss is seen after a delay). In this case, we see a major effect of a hippocampal removal, because it disrupts critical memory circuits connecting the medial temporal region to areas of the left cerebral cortex outside the anterior temporal region. We shall see a further application of this model when we consider the effects of right hippocampal lesions on spatial memory.

VISUAL MEMORY FUNCTION OF THE RIGHT TEMPORAL LOBE

Whereas patients with right temporal-lobe lesions typically obtain normal scores on verbal memory tasks, they show a highly predictable impairment in memory for complex visual patterns. Thus, if they are allowed to study briefly a set of a dozen photographs of unfamiliar faces (such as one might find in a college yearbook) and are then asked to select those faces again from a larger group about ninety seconds later, such patients make many errors, whilst patients with left temporal-lobe lesions find the task easy and obtain normal scores. The impairment is not specific to faces but applies also to the recognition of nonsense patterns that cannot be coded readily in words. The right temporal-lobe patients do indeed try to overcome their handicap by verbal analysis of the salient features, but verbal coding cannot provide an adequate representation of such a complex and idiosyncratic pattern as a particular human face.

The impairment in memory for visual patterns seen in patients who have undergone a right temporal lobectomy has its parallel in the monkey, where bilateral removal of the inferior temporal cortex causes a lasting impairment in visual pattern recognition. We are thus dealing with a specialization of the temporal neocortex, with the added feature that in human beings the right temporal cortex plays a more important role that the left, so that even a unilateral lesion in the right hemisphere causes a profound deficit. Moreover, such deficits are not exacerbated by inclusion of the hippocampal region in the right temporal lobectomy, since the critical cortical area is already compromised.

RIGHT HIPPOCAMPAL CONTRIBUTION TO SPATIAL MEMORY

There remain certain other learning and memory tasks on which deficits are seen after right temporal lobectomy if, and only if, there has been an extensive removal from the hippocampal region. With rare exceptions, these tasks involve spatial memory, as assessed not only by maze-learning ability but also by the accuracy with which the position of objects in space can be recalled.

Most mammals, from rat to human beings, are remarkably efficient at remembering the location of objects in their environment. This is a biologically useful accomplishment, enabling the organism to avoid sources of danger and return to sources of food, as well as, at the human level, helping us to know where to look for objects and information that we may suddenly need. An unusual feature of this kind of memory is that it is achieved without any deliberate intention to remember. There are now numerous studies in normal subjects showing that people take note automatically of the position of objects in the external world and can recall this information just as well when they did not know that memory would be tested as when they were forewarned. For this reason, when Mary Lou Smith and I decided to test the recall of object location in patients with various brain lesions, we used a so-called incidental-learning task, in which the subjects were not aware that memory would be tested, and then we went on to replicate our findings under intentional-learning conditions. In both cases, accuracy of recall was found to be dependent upon the integrity of the right hippocampal region.

The experimental setup used is illustrated in Figure 10, which

Figure 10. Object-location recall task: representative arrangement of the toy objects in the sixteen fixed locations (*Reproduced by permission of Pergamon Press, Oxford*).

shows an array of sixteen toy objects randomly distributed in fixed locations on a square board.[14] In the incidental-learning condition, subjects were told that this was a test of their ability to estimate prices and that they would be required to estimate the average price of the real object represented by each toy. They were to point to each object in turn, name it, and then be prepared to estimate the price at the end of ten seconds. This was to ensure that due attention was paid to each object and that all subjects had an equal exposure to the array.

Upon completion of the pricing task, the array was screened from view, and the subjects were asked to recall as many of the names of the objects as they could. They were then presented with all sixteen objects and instructed to replace them on the board in exactly the same position that they had occupied before. The error in recall of location was measured by the mean displacement of the objects from their original positions.

The patients tested included two right temporal-lobe groups, one (RTh) with small hippocampal excisions and one (RTH) with extensive removals from the hippocampal zone, as well as the corresponding left temporal-lobe groups (LTh and LTH). In addition, a left frontal-lobe group and a right frontal-lobe group participated in the study; they consisted of patients who had undergone a unilateral excision from the frontal cortex, also for the relief of epilepsy.

None of the patient groups was impaired in the immediate recall of the objects, but, when asked to replace the objects in their original positions, the RTH group demonstrated a striking impairment in the recall of location, their mean displacement error being at least twice as large as that of any of the other groups.

Although this finding clearly implicated the right hippocampal region in the performance of this task, it left open the question of whether the deficit would have appeared if recall had been truly immediate, instead of after a four-minute delay during which object recall was tested. To settle this question, Smith carried out a further experiment in which the objects were swept off the board the instant the last one had been priced, and the subject was immediately requested to replace them in their original positions. Under these conditions, the RTH group performed just as well as the normal control group. The results of this and related experiments have led us to conclude that patients with radical right hippocampal excisions can encode the locations of objects normally but show abnormally rapid forgetting of this information over the ensuing few minutes.

Thus our examination of the memory changes resulting from unilateral anterior temporal-lobe lesions has reaffirmed the important contribution made by the hippocampus to the retention of new information beyond the immediate present but has also highlighted the role of hemispheric specialization in determining on which tasks deficits would appear. It seems to me unlikely that these differential effects of left and right hippocampal lesions reflect any intrinsic specialization of the hippocampus, but rather that they are due to the strong anatomical connections linking each hippocampus to the neocortex of the same hemisphere.

FRONTAL LOBES AND THE TEMPORAL ORGANIZATION OF MEMORY

Although we still know little about how long-term memories are represented in the brain, the posterior cortex is more likely to be implicated than the frontal lobes. We have just seen that patients

with frontal-lobe lesions of either hemisphere showed good retention of the position of objects in an array after a single exposure
to them. Such patients have also been shown to have normal scores
on various verbal memory tasks that give trouble to patients with
left temporal-lobe lesions. Nevertheless, there are some memory
tasks that they fail, and typically they are those tasks in which the
interfering effects of previous trials can impair present performance.[15] It is almost as though they cannot segregate irrelevant
items in memory and give salience to the immediately pertinent
information.

A famous experiment by Jacobsen in the monkey, carried out in
1935, illustrated the role of the frontal cortex in memory. The task
he used is known as delayed response, and in it the monkey is
confronted at the moment of choice with two identically covered
food-wells and must approach either the one on the left or the one
on the right on the basis of information received a few seconds
before. This predelay cue is the sight of the examiner placing a
morsel of food in one of the food-wells, both of which are at that
time out of the animal's reach. The two wells are then screened
from view for about five seconds, after which the screen is raised
and the tray bearing the food-wells pushed forward for the monkey
to make its choice. Since the position of the baited food-well varies
at random from trial to trial, the monkey has to suppress the
memory of previous trials and base its choice solely on what happened a few seconds before. Normal monkeys perform this task
very efficiently, as do animals with bilateral lesions of the temporal
neocortex, but Jacobsen found that after bilateral frontal lobectomy the monkeys' performance fell to chance, and subsequent
research has indicated a critical area in the lateral mid-frontal
cortex, bilateral removal of which causes lasting impairment on
this seemingly simple task.

The traditional delayed-response method does not lend itself
well to the study of human frontal-lobe function, because even
long delays can be bridged by verbal rehearsal of the response to
be made. However, one of my former students, Lilli Prisko,
adapted Konorski's delayed-comparison technique to bring out
deficits after frontal lobectomy in patients undergoing unilateral
cortical excisions for the relief of epilepsy: this task also embodied
an intratrial delay as an essential feature, but the items to be

remembered could not easily be verbalized. In Prisko's procedure, two easily discriminable stimuli in the same sensory modality (for example, two lights flashing at different frequencies) are presented in succession sixty seconds apart, and the subject has to say whether the second stimulus was the same as, or different from, the first. Patients with frontal-lobe lesions, unlike those with temporal-lobe lesions, were impaired on those tasks in which a few stimuli recurred in different pairings throughout the test, but they made virtually no errors on the one task in which new stimuli were used on each trial. This contrast supports the notion that patients with frontal-lobe lesions have a heightened susceptibility to the effects of preceding trials, rather than an inability to retain information over a short time interval.

RECENCY DISCRIMINATION

Prisko's results suggested to me that the frontal-lobe lesion had interfered with the patients' ability to keep the various trials apart, and hence that in the absence of other contextual cues they were less able than normal subjects to distinguish a stimulus presented only sixty seconds ago from ones presented earlier in the same series of trials. If, as has been proposed, items in memory normally carry time-tags that permit the discrimination of the more from the less recent, then it seemed possible that this time-marking process might be disturbed by frontal-lobe injury, so that serial-order judgments were impaired.

Subsequent work by Corsi, using three tasks that embodied different kinds of stimulus material (concrete words, representational drawings, and abstract paintings), has provided direct evidence that frontal-lobe lesions can impair the temporal ordering of recent events. On these recency-discrimination tasks, subjects were shown a long series of cards in fairly rapid succession, each card bearing two stimulus-items; whenever a question mark appeared between the items (as in Figure 11), the subject had to indicate which of the two items had been seen more recently. Usually both items had been shown before (say, eight cards ago as compared with thirty-two), but, in the limiting condition, one of them was new, in which case the task reduced to a simple test of recognition memory. Patients with temporal-lobe lesions showed mild deficits on the recognition measures (verbal after left tempo-

Figure 11. Recency-discrimination task: representational drawings. Sample test card. The subject must point to the item he or she saw more recently. (*Reproduced by permission of Springer-Verlag, Berlin*).

ral lobectomy, nonverbal after right) but no impairment of recency discrimination as such. In contrast, patients with frontal-lobe lesions could distinguish normally between material that had been presented before and material that was new, but they were impaired in judging the relative recency of two previously seen items. These findings point to some separability of the processes mediating item memory and memory for temporal order.

The results obtained with these three tasks not only confirmed the notion that frontal-lobe lesions impair recency discrimination, but they also indicated some specialization of function related to the side of the lesion. Patients with left frontal-lobe lesions showed a moderate deficit when the stimuli to be ordered were verbal but were unimpaired on either of the pictorial tasks. In contrast, patients with right frontal-lobe lesions were totally unable to judge the relative recency of the abstract paintings (performing at, or near, chance level) and were also impaired on recency judgments for representational drawings. On the verbal task, their performance was only slightly better than that of the left frontal-lobe group. Thus, in addition to material-specific effects related to the side of the lesion, these results point to a greater participation of the right frontal lobe than the left in recency discrimination. If indeed the right hemisphere is dominant for visually guided attention, as many people have suggested, then one might expect the right frontal lobe to be more critically involved than the left in a task that calls for the monitoring of a rapid sequence of externally ordered events.

How recency judgments are achieved is still a matter for debate. In Corsi's experiments, every other card was a test card, requiring an active search through memory for the items to be compared, and at first sight it may seem reasonable to suppose that the recency judgments would be based on the relative salience, or strength, of the representations in memory of the two items to be compared. There are, however, serious obstacles in the way of a strength theory of recency discrimination, since many factors other than recency normally contribute to the strength of a memory trace; these factors include duration, intensity, familiarity, and emotional significance, to name but a few. It therefore seems necessary to postulate some more direct encoding of temporal information as the basis of recency discrimination.

The importance of temporal coding in normal memory is now explicitly recognized, and much research effort is being devoted to the processes underlying it. Meanwhile, the analysis of impairments in the temporal organization of memory after specific brain lesions in human beings and other mammals is continuing to provide evidence for a major contribution from the frontal cortex to this dimension of behavior.

DISCUSSION

Q: *When or how does present memory become historic memory? Is this an interesting question or one whose answer is well known?*

A: I don't think that memory has to go through a series of stages and filters necessarily. In fact, there is quite a bit of evidence to show that information is built up through a number of systems acting in parallel, with some scope for interaction. But I think inner reflection and rehearsal play an important role in the establishment and maintenance of the long-term, really enduring memories. And here the conscious cognitive memory system is crucial in permitting us to refresh our old concepts by linking them to new experience. Here it has been instructive to follow a patient of Dr. Wilder Penfield's right from the time of the operation that resulted in amnesia, and to discover that his answers to questions of general knowledge became more imprecise over the years, as though we ordinarily give a little boost to our old semantic knowledge by reactivation of it according to what we read in the newspapers or discuss with others.

There was also a question earlier about why an excessive amount of alcohol causes memory loss, and it seems to me there are two possible meanings to this question. If you mean to ask, as I think you do, why it is that sometimes if you go out and really drink a lot of alcohol, you cannot the next day remember what happened the night before, then I think that the answer is probably that alcohol in large quantities impairs the activity of the cortex as a whole, so that it is doing much more than blocking the hippocampal memory system. If you test the intelligence of people (to say nothing of their motor skill), while they are imbibing all this alcohol, you will find very grave generalized impairments. But if someone has in mind the further question of why chronic memory impairments are sometimes found in habitual heavy drinkers (as in the so-called Korsakoff syndrome), then that is now recognized to be due to vitamin deficiency, in particular, to thiamine deficiency, brought about by poor dietary habits and is not a direct effect of alcohol itself. The vitamin deficiency results in damage to critical structures in the diencephalon that are also part of the cognitive memory system.

Q: *How old is HM? Does he know that he doesn't know?*

A: There seem to be quite a few more questions about HM. First, a simple one: He is 58. I used to go around referring to him as "this young man," but I have stopped saying that now after studying him all these years. The next question is interesting: The answer is yes: he knows that he doesn't know. It is characteristic of all the patients I have seen with bilateral medial temporal-lobe damage that they have insight into their condition. In addition, HM's operation had been discussed as a possibility for several years before it actually took place, and so, despite his retrograde amnesia, he now realizes that he has had the operation and that, because of it, he has a bad memory. He also reasons logically from that premise. For example, when he was still living with his mother, she did not like to leave him alone in the house, because, if a salesman or other stranger came to the door, HM would reason that, although he himself did not recognize the man, this was probably because of his own bad memory and the man might really be a friend of his mother's. So he would invite the person in, and when the mother came home she would find a stranger sitting in her living room.

HM's awareness of his memory impairment also expresses itself in frequent feelings of anxiety. Thus, I found when testing him that he was all right as long as he was working on a problem, but during the short interval between tests he would become visibly anxious and would say that he was worried lest he had done or said something inappropriate that he could not remember. At such times he would describe his subjective experience as being "like waking from a dream."

I have also been asked about another operation where the negative findings are in fact a little surprising. I have been asked what change in brain function one might expect to see after a bilateral cingulotomy, which is an operation sometimes performed in cases of intractable pain. It consists in interrupting a bundle of nerve fibers connecting the frontal lobes to various structures on the medial aspect of the hemispheres, but numerous other pathways entering and leaving the frontal lobes are spared. Some time ago Dr. Suzanne Corkin, working in the laboratory of the late Professor Teuber at MIT, examined a series of patients before and after this procedure, and, despite her expectation of finding cognitive deficits, she was quite unable to demonstrate any postoperative impairments. This does not, of course, mean that the bundle of fibers that was interrupted had no function, but rather that this lesion would have to be seen in combination with some other critical lesion before one could guess what that function might be.

I have also been asked a question that frequently comes up when I discuss observations made in epileptic patients. It is the question of how valid it is to extrapolate from patients who are having seizures to normal subjects. Now obviously all patient populations have certain built-in disadvantages, but where there is convergence of findings across different populations I think we are on pretty safe ground. So I would just point out that, wherever we have seen damage to the medial structures of the temporal lobes, the same memory deficits have been observed. This includes cases of naturally occurring illness, such as herpes encephalitis or damage to blood vessels or invasion by tumor tissue, as well as the evidence from the surgery for epilepsy. So I don't feel that we have to worry too much on that score.

NOTES

1. W. B. Scoville and B. Milner, "Loss of recent memory after bilateral hippocampal lesions," *Journal of Neurology, Neurosurgery and Psychiatry* 20 (1957), pp. 11–21. See also W. Penfield and B. Milner, "The memory deficit produced by bilateral lesions in the hippocampal zone," *A.M.A. Archives of Neurology and Psychiatry* 58 (1958), pp. 477–97.
2. M. Mishkin, "A memory system in the monkey," *Philosophical Transactions of the Royal Society of London* B299 (1982), pp. 85–95.
3. W. James, *Principles of Psychology*, vol. 1 (New York: Holt, Rinehart and Winston, 1890), pp. 646–48.
4. B. Milner, "Les troubles de la mémoire accompagnant des lésions hippocampiques bilatérales," in *Physiologie de l'Hippocampe* (Paris: C.N.R.S., 1962), pp. 257–72. (English translation in *Cognitive Processes and the Brain*, ed. P. M. Milner and Glickman (Princeton: Van Nostrand, 1965), pp. 97–111).
5. E. K. Warrington and L. Weiskrantz, "New method of testing long-term retention with special reference to amnesic patients," *Nature* 217 (1968), pp. 972–74. See also B. Milner, S. Corkin, and H.-L. Teuber, "Further analysis of the hippocampal amnesic syndrome," *Neuropsychologia* 6 (1968), pp. 267–82.
6. R. Diamond and P. Rozin, "Activation of existing memories in anterograde amnesia," *Journal of Abnormal Psychology* 93 (1984), pp. 98–105. See also P. Graf, L. R. Squire, and G. Mandler, "The information that amnesic patients do not forget," *Journal of Experimental Psychology* 10 (1984), pp. 164–78.
7. N. Cohen and L. R. Squire, "Preserved learning and retention of pattern analyzing skill in amnesia: dissociation of knowing how and knowing that," *Science* 218 (1980), pp. 207–9.
8. E. Tulving, "Episodic and semantic memory," in *Organization of Memory* ed. E. Tulving and W. Donaldson (New York: Academic Press, 1972), pp. 381–403.
9. T. Rasmussen and B. Milner, "Clinical and surgical studies of the cerebral speech areas in man," in *Cerebral Localization*, ed. K. J. Zulch, O. Creutzfeldt,

and G. C. Galbraith (Berlin: Springer-Verlag, 1975) pp. 238–57. For further discussion of the speech areas, see also T. Rasmussen and B. Milner, "The role of early left brain injury in determining lateralization of cerebral speech functions," *Annals of the New York Academy of Sciences* 299 (1977), pp. 355–69.

10. B. B. Murdock, Jr., "The serial position effect in free recall," *Journal of Experimental Psychology* 64 (1962), pp. 482–88. For cross-species comparisons, see also A. A. Wright, H. C. Santiago, S. F. Sands, D. F. Kendrick, and R. G. Cook, "Memory processing of serial lists by pigeons, monkeys, and people," *Science* 229 (1985), pp. 287–89.

11. N. J. Slamecka and P. Graf, "The generation effect: Delineation of a phenomenon," *Journal of Experimental Psychology: Human Learning and Memory* 4 (1978), pp. 592–604.

12. F. I. M. Craik and R. S. Lockhart, "Levels of processing: a framework for memory research," *Journal of Verbal Learning and Verbal Behavior* 11 (1972), pp. 671–84.

13. G. W. Van Hoesen, "The parahippocampal gyrus: new observations regarding its cortical connections in the monkey," *Trends in Neurosciences* 5 (1982), pp. 345–49.

14. M. L. Smith and B. Milner, "The role of the right hippocampus in the recall of spatial location," *Neuropsychologia* 19 (1981), pp. 781–93. The procedure was adapted from J. M. Mandler, D. Seegmiller, and J. Day, "On the coding of spatial information," *Memory and Cognition* 5 (1977), pp. 10–16.

15. For recent reviews of human frontal-lobe function, see B. Milner and M. Petrides, "Behavioural effects of frontal-lobe lesions in man," *Trends in Neurosciences* 7 (1984), pp. 403–7, and B. Milner, M. Petrides, and M. L. Smith, "Frontal lobes and the temporal organization of memory," *Human Neurobiology* (in press).

3. Modeling Memory and Learning

ROGER C. SCHANK AND COLLEEN M.
SEIFERT

The answer is artificial intelligence. What's the question?

This rubric seems to head the latest popular press releases. What is artificial intelligence, and why do we hear so much about it?

One reason for this increased popular interest in AI is the sudden advent of the personal computer. Out there in the world are lots of companies born in garages who would like nothing better than for you to own a personal computer. No one is quite sure what people are going to do with them, but they want you to own one and become "computer literate." In fact, there are plenty of people out there who are willing to teach you to become computer literate—for a fee. However, those of us who work in artificial intelligence are interested in getting computers to a point at which you don't have to be computer literate. Instead, our computers will be "people literate."

That's what artificial intelligence is about, though it didn't start out as a mission to make computers easy for people to deal with. Those of us who work in AI care about getting a machine to be able to act like a person—to talk, understand, solve problems. So, suppose we are going to build a machine that is really smart. Suppose HAL, the talking computer in 2001 and 2010, or R2-D2, the little robot in *Star Wars,* really existed. Most people who see these movies squirm in their seats because they are afraid machines like these might someday exist. The few people who squirm because they can't figure out how to build them are AI people. The future AI researchers are the ones who watch 2001 and say, "Gee, I wonder how we would do any of that!"

TEACHING LANGUAGE TO COMPUTERS

The problem of language was an obvious starting point, because computers in the future all speak. In fact, HAL and all the other smart computers not only speak but understand perfectly everything that you say. How is it that people can speak and understand so effortlessly? Understanding language is a complicated process for human beings, and for computers it has proved to be very difficult. Though you are reading this text and presumably understanding it, no computer is capable of doing so at this time. Although we have made some strides in artificial intelligence, its successes have been exaggerated by the media, and consequently people believe that we've solved all the problems in the field. We haven't, but we have learned something about identifying the problems.

Take the common word *take*. We need to give the computer a definition of the word *take* such that it can recognize and understand the appropriate meaning whenever the word occurs. This doesn't sound very hard; that is, we all know what *take* means. But let's take at look at *take* as it appears in these sentences:

John took the bus.
John took the candy.
John took a punch.
John took it easy.
John took a nap.
John took a letter.
John took his temperature.
John took his time.

Now, since you surely know how to program, write into your computer the dictionary definition you'd like your computer to have for the word *take*.

When you take a bus, is that the same as when you take candy? When you take candy, you own it and are about to eat it. This is not true of buses; when you take a bus, you ride on it. And when you take a nap, you don't actually "take" a nap at all. There is no such thing as a nap; you just sleep. When you take it easy, you haven't taken "it" anywhere; there is no "it." *It* doesn't refer to anything. When you take a punch, you presumably haven't done something you wanted to do at all. And when you take your temperature—let's not even start on that one.

Verbs aren't the only words that suffer from this problem. For example, consider the word *hand* in these sentences:

John needs a hand.
Give John a hand.
John asked his sweetheart for her hand.
John raised his hand.
John is an old hand.
John had a hand in the cookie jar.
John had a hand in the robbery.

Take those last two: They look so similar, yet in one case you might assume John is a child and, in the other, an accomplice to a theft. How do you know that hands in cookie jars are likely to belong to children? In addition, *hand* has the delightful property of being a verb in some contexts, such as in "hand it over." So, what do you teach a computer about *hand*? When is it a noun; when is it a verb; and when should it make you think of small children?

The problem we're having is that language is much more than the sum of its parts. What if we could teach a computer all the words in the English language? The early attempts to do this involved putting dictionaries into the computer, that is, representing each word and its meaning in the machine. However, dictionaries didn't provide solutions to problems with sentences like those we've just seen. Storing all the possible ways to use *take* under its word definition proved to be unworkable. You can't just look up the right meaning for each word and expect to arrive at the true meaning of a sentence. This is because languages have the property of allowing you to say much more than the words themselves imply. A small change to a sentence, such as changing the object, can deeply affect the meaning of the statement and the conclusions you draw from it. For example, consider these few sentences, and think about what each implies about the world:

John hit Mary.
John hit his child.
John hit his teacher.
John hit a policeman.
John hit Muhammad Ali.

When you see that John hit Mary, you start worrying about Mary, and you wonder why John is such a brute. Do you feel that way when John hits Muhammad Ali? You start worrying about John!

How are we going to teach a machine when to worry about John? The structure of the two sentences is identical, but something very different is going on in terms of their meaning. There is much more information involved in sentences than is apparent from the words used. As another example, consider the following boring little story:

John went to a restaurant. He ordered lobster. He left a small tip. He left.

What did John eat? Lobster, right? Where is that mentioned in the story? Who served him the lobster? The waitress, right? Again, that does not appear in the story. Was John happy with the service? No. This information comes from a sentence that says something quite different—that he left a small tip. The story does not provide a connection between the tip and the service for us—we have to make the necessary connections from our knowledge about the world of restaurants.

What we learn from these examples is that the problem in teaching computers to understand language isn't language at all. The problem in teaching computers to understand language is *knowledge*. We have to teach the computer, not just language, but also what we know about the world.

ORGANIZING KNOWLEDGE IN MEMORY

Some of our knowledge about the world is organized in memory as "scripts." A script is a collection of little things you know about life that are so mundane and boring that you can't imagine talking about them, but you can expect that your hearer knows the same scripts and can therefore refer to the information implicitly. So if a machine is going to understand the story of John and the restaurant, we have to teach the machine the *restaurant script*. We have to teach it that when you go into a restaurant you sit down, you read a menu, you order food, what you order is what you eat, somebody brings you the food, you pay that person, you may leave the person a tip for good service, and so on. In fact, if you start writing down everything you know about going to a restaurant, you discover you know a great deal about it. There is, in fact, a lot to know about restaurants.

Now that we can teach the machine about scripts, will it be able to understand the way people do? About ten years ago those of us in the Yale AI project wrote a computer program that processed stories using scripts. The input to the program was stories from the newspaper, and the program was designed to understand the stories and produce summaries or translations of them. Here is an example story about a car accident that appeared in the *New Haven Register:*

Friday evening a car swerved off Route 69. The vehicle struck a tree. The passenger, a New Jersey man, was killed. David Hall, 27, was pronounced dead at the scene by Dana Blanchard, Medical Examiner. Frank Miller, 32, 593 Foxon Road, the driver, was taken to Milford Hospital by Flanagan Ambulance. He was treated and released. No charges were made. Patrolman Robert Onophrio investigated the accident.

The computer program processed this story and produced this summary:

An automobile hit a tree near Highway 69 four days ago. David Hall, age 27, residence in New Jersey, the passenger, died. Frank Miller, age 32, residence 593 Foxon Road in New Haven, Connecticut, the driver, was slightly injured. The police department did not file charges.

As you can see from the summary, the program is not just spitting back the language from the input but has understood the information in a different way. The program can answer questions posed in English: "Was anyone killed?" It answers, "Yes, David Hall died." "Was anyone hurt?" "Yes, Frank Miller was slightly injured." These answers are produced by using the knowledge encoded in the car accident script to understand the input information. For example, the input story says that "Frank Miller was treated and released from the hospital." The accident script says that if you get hurt, you'll be taken to a hospital, and if you're not very badly hurt, you'll be released. The program then makes the inference that Frank Miller was only slightly injured.

Programs like this one met with some success in understanding stories as people do. Other programs were developed to use scripts based on knowledge of different contexts. One program simulated a U.S. senator by using a script to answer questions as a senator would answer them. It had a right-wing script and a left-wing script and could arrive at different interpretations of events depending on which script was used. A third program read the UPI news wire, using scripts, and could summarize and answer questions about a variety of stories, from earthquakes to terrorists.

Although it seemed we were on the right track toward getting computers to understand, we ran into two problems. The first, that our programs didn't know *enough,* is best demonstrated by the examples that follow. The second, that our programs were not like people in a very fundamental way, will be the subject of the rest of this chapter.

In fact, our programs did understand car accidents, and a few other things. But there is a huge gap between what the programs could understand and what they needed to understand. This gap is best illustrated by examining some of the failures in understanding that our programs suffered. My favorite example is a program designed to make up stories of the kind you might invent for a child. The program created a small world of living and talking animals who had their own society and interacted in certain ways. Once the setting was established, the characters acted out the behaviors they knew about, and a story resulted. We gave these animals their own scripts, goals, and plans for living, and hoped it was enough knowledge to let them function in their world. Some of the stories that came out showed very clearly where the knowledge we had put into the program was lacking.

One day Joe Bear was hungry. He asked his friend Irving Bird where some honey was. Irving told him there was a beehive in the oak tree. Joe threatened to hit Irving if he didn't tell him where some honey was.

Our program had to have quite a bit of intelligence to generate this story, but it obviously didn't understand what it had created. It didn't know that Irving had told Joe where the honey was. To solve this particular problem, we had to add the information that beehives contain honey:

One day Joe Bear was hungry. He asked his friend Irving Bird where some honey was. Irving told him there was a beehive in the oak tree. Joe walked to the oak tree. He ate the beehive.

We needed another quick fix to inform the computer that you should take the edible honey out of the beehive before consuming it. But though it's easy enough to fix these problems, you always have to wonder where the next trouble spot lies. The following is an example of another kind of trouble we ran into. Since the stories were about a main character, the program had no concept of "noticing" what another character had done.

Henry Ant was thirsty. He walked over to the riverbank where his good friend Bill Bird was sitting. Henry slipped and fell into the river. He wasn't able to call for help. He drowned.

This story is all right, but it's not the story the program intended to tell, because the main character unexpectedly died in the middle of it. Since Bill was not asked a direct question, he didn't notice his friend drowning next to him. "Noticing" was changed to an inference made from any change in location, allowing Bill to respond to Henry's fall.

This story had another problem: Representing the idea of drowning is quite difficult. So far, the program has rules that say that people drown if they fall into water and can't ask for help. This representation of drowning was inadequate, so next, we added the idea of gravity pulling an animal down ("X fell" became "gravity moved X") and the opportunity for friends to help if one calls out for help.

Henry Ant was thirsty. He walked over to the riverbank where his good friend Bill Bird was sitting. Henry slipped and fell into the river. Gravity drowned.

Poor gravity didn't have any friends, and certainly couldn't call out for help, and was firmly located in the river, according to our representation. No wonder it drowned.

Next, we tried to get the program to understand and generate Aesop's fables. You may recognize which fable we are attempting to generate:

Once upon a time there was a dishonest fox and a vain crow. One day the crow was sitting in a tree holding a piece of cheese in his mouth. He noticed he was holding the piece of cheese. He became hungry and swallowed the cheese. The fox walked over to the crow.

The program doesn't have enough information to make the story come out right. It had a piece of knowledge that said, "If you are an animal and you see food, eat it." We got around this rule temporarily by starting with Henry having just eaten. But soon another of our seemingly reasonable rules ran into trouble. This one was, "If you become very hungry and don't get fed for some time, you get sick."

One day Henry Crow was sitting in his tree holding a piece of cheese in his mouth when up came Bill Fox. Bill saw the cheese and was hungry. He said, "Henry, I like your singing very much. Won't you please sing for me?" Henry, flattered by the compliment, began to sing. The cheese fell to the ground. Bill Fox saw the cheese on the ground and was very hungry. He became sick.

The story gets worse as it goes on from there. We now have Henry in the tree, the cheese on the ground, and Bill out of the action. However, we also have a rule that if you want something, you must go through a certain procedure to decide who owns it and what you can do to get it. such as bargain for it or offer to pay for it, or whatever, depending on your relationship to the character who owns it. This routine for obtaining objects makes sense as a definition of how to proceed, but unfortunately it too has its problems:

Henry Crow saw the cheese on the ground and he became hungry. He knew that he owned the cheese. He felt pretty honest with himself, so he decided not to trick himself into giving up the cheese. He wasn't trying to deceive himself either, nor did he feel competitive with himself. He remembered he was also in a position of dominance over himself so he refused to give himself the cheese. He couldn't think of a good reason why he should give himself the cheese because if he did that he would lose the cheese. So he offered to bring himself a worm if he'd give himself the cheese. That sounded okay but he didn't know where any worms were. So he said to himself, "Henry, do you know where any worms are?"

Here's a nice example of a crow finding himself in an infinite loop.

So, the first point is that computers have to have a lot of knowledge. Now, AI researchers can sit down and try to pack all that knowledge into a computer and try to fix all the problems that causes. But there's a second problem with this script-based approach that became clear after some of these programs had been developed. We had programs that understood car accident stories, earthquake stories, stories about war, and all sorts of situations for which one could write mundane scripts. We used to demonstrate these programs for incoming visitors, and we showed the same ten stories over and over. After about the one hundred fiftieth time of seeing these stories processed and understood, we were bored. The same story was being processed over and over again. The question is, Why isn't the machine bored?

Does that seem like a silly question? It seemed that the machine should have been really tired of this story and should have said, "If I have to read about that earthquake in Italy one more time, I'm going to get sick." But it never did that; in fact, it didn't even know it had read that story before. What was wrong with the programs the Yale researchers had developed? Not only didn't they remember, but in a serious sense they didn't really understand. We had defined understanding as the ability to simulate input and output behavior. Therefore, to understand a story was to paraphrase it, or answer questions about it, or translate it. Even though some programs were fairly successful at doing these behaviors, their failure to remember pointed out that they did not really understand as people do. The problem of memory and learning, a crucial part of understanding, was left out of our theories. And though we didn't set out to simulate how people remember, memory became the focus of our attempts to get programs to understand.

REMINDING AND LEARNING

How do people remember old experiences and learn from new ones? One phenomenon that sheds light on both the problem of retrieval and our ability to learn is the phenomenon of reminding. Reminding is an everyday occurrence, a common feature of memory. We are reminded of one person by another, of one building by another, and so on. But, more significantly, one event can remind you of another. Imagine the following situation:

You've been to McDonald's many, many times, but I find out that you've never been to Burger King. I tell you, "Boy, are you in for a treat! I'm going to take you to Burger King." So we drive off to Burger King, and we stand in line and order hamburgers and put them on our trays and pay and go sit down and eat. And you say to me, "You know, this place reminds me of McDonald's."

From your reminding, it's clear that you've understood Burger King in a profound way. You understand Burger King in terms of McDonald's because they share many features. You go in Burger King, and you have to stand in line (just as in McDonald's and lots of other places). Then, you give the cashier your order (again just as in McDonald's). Then, you pay for your food before you sit down and eat it (McDonald's again!).

In fact, the two experiences share so many features that you can't help remembering one when you first experience the other. These shared features form the basis of a mental framework or knowledge structure in memory. And because our two restaurants share these features, both restaurants would be stored under the same structure in memory. Understanding one experience means accessing the same structure in memory that the other shares. Most of the time this is useful in understanding things in the world. We can't help thinking about related memories as we try to understand our experiences. But occasionally, this property gets in the way, as it did in this experience:

My father, who is a fairly old man, decided he would like to visit his boyhood home in a small town called Mountaindale, New York. We drove to Mountaindale to visit the house he had lived in, and the people currently living there were kind enough to show us around. My father asked the woman who lived there where she worked. I could see why he was thinking about this, as Mountaindale is a very small town, and he didn't really understand where you could get a job, especially since he lived there in 1918 or so. She said she worked in Monticello, a bigger town about fifteen miles away. My father said, "Monticello! How could you possibly work in Monticello and live in Mountaindale?" Now, my father is not an unintelligent man, and he in fact had just been on the freeway that connects Mountaindale with Monticello. But he couldn't understand how you could possibly make this trip. The reason is that when he lived in Mountaindale, there were no cars, little money, and lots of horses. The only way he could ever get from Mountaindale to Monticello was by horse. He was looking at the world through 1918 glasses, even though he had arrived via a 1984 freeway five minutes earlier. During the visit, he was imagining and understanding the world in 1918 terms. He was asking where the brook was, where the barn was, where the trees had gone; all the things of interest to him were from that 1918 frame of reference.

When we understand something, we understand it in terms of a limited framework you might call a "domain." The domain contains a set of expectations about the world and a set of beliefs that certain things will occur in a particular order. The insight in scripts was that we have these expectations about events like restaurants and car accidents linked together in packages of information that can be recalled from memory as a set. But the failure of scripts was that they couldn't change over time, with new experiences. Though it's sometimes possible to view the world from the 1918 framework, you are actually changing and updating your scripts constantly. Each time you change a script you are adding new knowledge about what you expect from the world; in other words, you are learning. Even the familiar restaurant script is subject to change, as this experience shows:

I once gave a talk at General Motors, and when lunchtime came they took me to the company cafeteria to eat. It turns out that the actions in the cafeteria were not quite like those in a restaurant. You can't just verbally order your meal from a waitress, but you must write down your order on a check. This seemed a bit odd to me, and I filed it away somewhere in memory. A year later, I went to Bell Laboratories and the same thing happened to me. And I was reminded of the experience at General Motors.

You might say, "So what? That happens to me all the time." But it never happened to the computer programs. Not once did they ever say, "You know, this story about an earthquake in Italy reminds me of that story about that earthquake in Yugoslavia," or, in fact, "reminds me of a plane crash in Yugoslavia." The ability to modify our scripts in response to experiences is critically important. This ability was lacking in our programs. What was missing was the ability to make new expectations and new generalizations, or, to put it another way, the ability to learn.

As a result of my Bell Labs and General Motors experiences, a codicil was added to my restaurant script to say, "Whenever you go to a company cafeteria, don't expect to give your order to a waitress, expect to write it down." That expectation may turn out to be wrong too. We are constantly generating all kinds of expectations, and we attempt to determine if they are right under new circumstances. That's how we learn, and the following story is my favorite example of this process:

X described how his wife would never make his steak as rare as he liked it. When this was told to Y, it reminded Y of a time, 30 years earlier, when he tried to get his hair cut in a short style in England, and the barber would not cut it as short as he wanted it.

The two experiences, the steak and the haircut, don't have a lot in common, and one took place thirty years before the other. In order for Y to be reminded of his experience, he had to hold this memory in his mind for thirty years, waiting to be recalled. In fact, Y said, when asked, that he hadn't thought about that experience in thirty years.

This question is to me the essence of what artificial intelligence is really about: Can you build an algorithm that would replicate that behavior and tell me what it would look like? Here's an attempt at sketching out the procedure that produces this reminding.

X is saying, "My steak is never cooked as rare as I'd like it by my wife." Y is now in the position of trying to understand that sentence. The first thing he does is bring in what we call a knowledge structure, that is, some package of information with built-in expectations, like those from the restaurant example. What knowledge structure would be useful here? This is a crucial question, because you have to bring in a knowledge structure that is general enough to contain other information. If you had a "wife cooking steak" knowledge structure, an obvious guess for how to organize this information in memory, you would never be reminded of the haircut. In other words, if you process something with a very narrow script, you'll never see the broader implications or make connections between steaks and haircuts.

A better candidate for the knowledge structure Y was using is a "somebody provides service for somebody else" knowledge structure. What expectations would be provided by such a structure? Probably that you ask someone to help you; if they feel it is appropriate for you to ask, and if they are capable of doing it, then they help you.

Assuming Y did have this type of structure in memory, what

would cause him to get to this particular experience? Once he had accessed the "provide service" structure, why did he also remember the experience at the barber? *Y* had to have been asking himself why. He had to have been trying to explain what had gone wrong in the steak example. The expectation about serving had failed, and now *Y* had to try to *explain* it. The failure in the steak example is that he expects his wife to do what he asks both because it was appropriate to ask her and because she was capable of doing it. Why didn't she? The explanation that *Y* constructed is clear from the reminding he had: The wife of *X* must have believed that it was inappropriate to do something that extreme. The explanation is the same as the one *Y* had about the haircut: The barber simply thought it was inappropriate to cut anyone's hair that short.

What does this reminding tell us about human memory? It tells us that for thirty years a little flag was waving around in *Y*'s head saying, "If you ever run into anything else in a *'provide service'* situation where somebody doesn't do something because it's too extreme, even though they could have done it, call me." The purpose of this kind of index into memory is to compare the next version of an expectation failure with the previous version, so that the expectation can be changed to avoid the failure in the future. By finding two instances in which expectations have failed in similar ways and the explanation is the same, you can compare the two cases for the common elements. The commonalities between the two cases then serve as the basis or motivation for forming a new structure.

Imagine that you've never been to either McDonald's or Burger King, but have been to lots of restaurants. The first time you go to McDonald's, you suffer many expectation failures from your restaurant script—you pay before eating, stand in line to order, and so on. It's not clear from the one exception what the important generalities are that make McDonald's a special case. After visiting Burger King, the two instances can be compared, and a new category, fast food restaurants, can be formed. By using two failures to form the generalization, the resulting changed knowledge structure will ignore features specific to one of them and concentrate on features they share, which are more likely to be related to the explanation of the failure.

"Understanding" means being reminded of the thing in memory that is closest to the experience you are currently processing. This principle is constantly demonstrated in the world:

As a public lecturer for years, I used to be infuriated with the person in the audience who said, "Isn't this just like the work of X?" I'd be mad. It wasn't like the work of X. How could they not see that? Now I say, "Ha! You've just proved my theory. You've understood what I said in terms of the things closest to it in your memory."

Remembering jokes fits in nicely with this theory of memory. The fact that people are sometimes reminded of a joke tells us something about jokes as well as about reminding. Jokes are relevant because they are frequently about people's unexpected behavior. Expectation failures are often the basis of something that strikes people as funny. To access jokes in our memories, we must have indexed them by their particular types of failures. We retrieve them again when we encounter a similar kind of failure. Here's an example of a reminding involving a joke:

X's daughter was diving for sand dollars. X pointed out where there were a great many sand dollars, but X's daughter continued to dive where she was. X asked why. She said that the water was shallower where she was diving. This reminded X of the joke about the drunk who was searching for his ring under the lamppost because the light was better there even though he had lost the ring elsewhere.

In this example, X perceives his daughter as failing to do what is expected at the plan level. This is recognized by examining her goal of finding sand dollars. We expect that she will look and get the sand dollars in the right place. When she fails to do this, we check our expectations about how to search to find where her problem lies. We know she does indeed have the goal of finding the dollars; we know she knows where to look, since X told her; and she has the ability to dive for them. The failure is in using the best strategy for searching: The girl seems to be using the easiest plan even though it is the plan with the least probability of success. This failure, together with the search context, provides the reminding of the drunk story as an example of the same phenomenon. Obviously, the joke must have been understood and stored in memory in terms of this expectation failure about planning.

Our conclusion, that we process new information in terms of old, points out the problems with the computer programs we saw.

These programs failed to make use of the experiences they had. When a program reads an earthquake story, it should be gathering expectations from all the other earthquake stories it has seen, watching for failures that might be shared, and drawing generalizations from them. For example, on reading twenty-seven stories about earthquakes in Italy, it should either come to the conclusion that Italy is very prone to earthquakes, or it should become bored. Experiences that exactly match previous episodes are boring; failures provoke interest, explanation, and learning.

THE EXPLANATION PROCESS

The problem of explanation is illustrated by this story:

X was walking along a beach in Puerto Rico at dusk when he noticed a sign on the beach saying "No swimming at this point." Yet everyone was swimming happily and it was clearly safe. X walked along farther and came upon a new sign saying "Don't go beyond this point. Dangerous!" X explained this to himself by assuming that the hotel had put up the signs to try to cover itself legally in case of an accident. At this point X was reminded of the signs in Connecticut that say *Road legally closed. Pass at your own risk,* when the road is in full use. X had previously explained these signs to himself by saying the state of Connecticut, in the event of an accident, wanted to be able to say the road was legally closed, and that, therefore, the state was not responsible.

Now why was X reminded of this? It seems obvious that X was reminded because that's what they were doing in Puerto Rico; that is, putting up a sign to cover themselves. Once X had explained the hotel signs as an attempt to cover any legal liability, the previous experience with the same explanation came to mind. Forming the explanation was useful in both cases in order to understand the experience. However, when the reminding occurred, the opportunity to make a new generalization came with it. From the two examples, X could add an expectation that institutions like states and hotels are likely to take such steps to protect themselves. From only one experience, it would be difficult to tell how far to generalize the expectation—To all states? To governments? To people who own roads? The role of the reminding is to help you make the appropriate generalizations. Having the second experience is quite functional in constraining and guiding the generalization.

This is roughly what is called the explanation process. The most important thing we do as understanders is to find anomalies in our own lives; that is, we look around for what is wrong, what is strange, what doesn't fit. We notice the things that are inconsistent with what is normally expected. We try to predict the actions of the people and institutions we have to deal with and the actions of the world around us. We constantly question ourselves, and when we find we don't know the answer, when things are anomalous, when things don't make sense, we devote some effort to explaining what is wrong.

What makes something anomalous? First, something is anomalous if it is something you wouldn't ordinarily do. Second, you know particular individuals and their patterns of behavior, and therefore know when they do something *they* wouldn't ordinarily do. You then consider other motivations: Maybe this has some result that would be good for them. Maybe it's part of some pattern of behavior that they're involved in that you don't know about. Maybe it's part of some greater plan they have. Maybe they believe something different about the world than you believe. And if none of these explanations help you understand it, then it is anomalous. We try to find the kind of explanation that will provide a solution to the problem for us.

In the explanation process, we are looking for generalizations that are both inclusive and instructive. Finding the right level at which to generalize is very important. Imagine you've bought a stock on the market and it goes up immediately. That's expectation failure of a successful sort. No one expects stock to go up immediately, so it would be nice to use this experience to help predict when, in fact, we can have this particular expectation. We want to learn from this experience, so what we need to do is to generalize over the right parameters. But what are the right parameters? You should always buy on Tuesday? You should always buy computer stocks? You should always buy stocks valued under twenty dollars, with a price–earnings ratio under ten? There are lots of parameters available, and what we try to do as learners is establish which parameters are most relevant. So, in the hotel example X had to decide that the most relevant parameter was protection of one's legal liability through signs.

Now the question is, How should you generalize the experience? How applicable is this rule for protecting liability? Should you put signs up all over your house? Where does this idea stop? If the state of Connecticut does the same thing as the hotel does, then you can form a generalization like "Large institutions put up signs, and you should distrust them." At this point, you may be reminded of STOP signs. Large institutions put those signs up—do they do so to protect themselves, or to protect people? Ultimately, one would assume that STOP signs are to protect people and therefore should not be ignored. Finally, the generalization can be constrained to "When you see that a large institution has put up a sign that might possibly be for its own legal protection, ignore it." And, in fact, that is what you'd have to do, or you'd never get to swim in Puerto Rico or drive in Connecticut.

Explanation is therefore very important in understanding and learning about the world. But we need to know both what to explain and what constitutes an explanation. How many and what kinds of explanations are there? And, once given an explanation, how do we decide it is satisfactory? Let's take a look at some examples to get an idea of the classes of possible explanations. Consider a situation in which a professor asks an advisee why he has not been working on his thesis lately. It is possible to concoct many different explanations. Each of these explanations would serve to cause the professor to update her model of this student in some way, that is, in a small sense, to learn something:

"Why aren't you working on your thesis?"

—"Because I had to celebrate my friend's birthday last night." People often explain themselves by giving a fact that contributed in some way to their behavior. This fact is an *excuse*.

—"Because I don't think it needs work." When someone does something that we had no reason to expect he would do, we try to find out why by trying to simulate his reasoning, to see whether he might have *alternative beliefs* we hadn't considered.

—"It is so hot that the paper keeps melting." Sometimes the reason we don't understand something is because of a *law of physics* that we don't know. We change our rules to correspond with experience and possibly prevent problems in the future.

—"Yale doesn't require one any more."
When we know that someone is playing according to externally defined rules, we can look for explanations of behavior in those *institutionalized rules.*

—"I've discovered that not writing it gets your professor to the point where she will sign anything."
There are a set of "tricks" for living that get people where they want to go. "Ask for advice," or "Never date the boss's daughter" are examples. These *rules of thumb* are often good explanations.

—"It's finished."
We want to learn about things in the world as well as people. We need to know about cats, dogs, cars, computers and so on. When we find a *new fact,* we try to classify it in a set of objects to make it more usable.

—"I didn't want to appear stupid in front of the other students."
People do things because of how they imagine it will make them look. They buy cars, dress, even marry, because it evokes an *appearance* in their own or others' minds that they would like to maintain.

—"Not writing it every other week is the best way to stay sane while writing."
We can explain the actions of others by understanding where the particular action that we do not understand fits within a broader *plan.* Saying that an action is a step in a coherent plan toward a goal explains that action.

—"Oh, you thought I wanted a Ph.D.!"
An action can be explained by connecting it to the *goal* it was intended to achieve. Knowing what someone wants is an important part of understanding.

—"I've quit school."
Knowing what *role theme* people are acting under tells us a lot about why they are doing what they are doing, and thus point-

ing out a role theme can be an explanation. That is, saying that someone is a doctor and that is what doctors do will serve as an explanation in some cases.

—"I just don't do that sort of thing."
Since *scripts* are fossilized plans, script explanations are just simpler versions of what we have for plans.

—"My wife is writing it for me."
Doing something for someone else does not require a coherent plan of action. It merely requires that you believe that someone you want to please wants something. It thus explains an action to say that the real explanation is that someone is an *agent* in someone else's plan.

—"Not working seemed the best thing to do at the time."
Sometimes people do things because they couldn't think of a better action. This *lack of alternative plan* is an "explain it away" explanation. It is sometimes the best we can do.

—"Lama Dama says that that which is not approached directly is first finished."
Not everyone shares the same belief system. Those who are religious or mystical may well believe *mystical laws* that are deemed inappropriate by others.

From this example, you can see that there are a wide variety of explanations possible for any anomaly, and that the selection of an explanation is a complicated process. As we discover more about how humans explain and learn about the world around them, we find new questions for researchers who try to teach a computer to do the same. Although this enterprise is very difficult, our ideas about knowledge organization and explanation are proving to be useful in programming our computers. Theories of explanation and reminding have given us clues about how to put computers on the road to understanding.

A COMPUTER UNDERSTANDING SPECTRUM

The basic hypothesis presented here is that in attempting to understand, we are attempting to relate our new experiences to our prior experiences. We do so by utilizing knowledge structures that organize those previous experiences. Understanding means being reminded of the closest prior experience in memory and being able to use the expectations generated by that reminding to help in processing the current experience.

Given this view of understanding, what will it mean for computers to understand? Will they be able to understand just as people do? Before we can answer this, we have to be able to make some distinctions about the nature of understanding. There are many levels of understanding, even between people. Certainly we can expect that computers will show differences in the ability to understand, just as people do. This diversity in understanding can be characterized as an understanding spectrum. There are three kinds of computer understanding: *making sense,* on the lower end, *cognitive understanding,* as a middle point, and *complete empathy,* at the higher end.

Computers can, at this moment, make sense of what they read. This is the level of understanding at which events that occur in the world can be interpreted by the understander in terms of a coherent (although incomplete) picture of how those events came to pass, despite the understander's lack of empathy with the actors involved. So, for example, it is possible to type in information from a UPI wire and get a summary of a newspaper story or a translation to another language. In that computers can now manipulate the symbols of language in an informed way, computers can at least make sense at this level.

But "understanding" in its extreme form can be defined as complete empathy, such as in the question of whether men and women can ever really understand each other. If "understand" can mean the level of empathy we are talking about when we ask, "Can a husband and wife ever understand each other?" how can you use "computer understanding" in the same sense? By definition, understanding consists of processing incoming experiences in terms of particular memories. Specifically, this means that people who have different goals, beliefs, expectations, and general lifestyles will understand identical episodes quite differently. In essence, then, no two people understand in exactly the same way or with the same result. Thus, men tend to understand certain classes of experiences differently than women. Complete empathy is the kind of understanding that might obtain between twins, very old friends who know each other's every mood and motivation, and other such combinations of people that exist only rarely in the world. Here's an example:

A: I was very upset by your actions last night.

B: I thought you might have been; it was a lot like the way you treated me last week.

A: But I meant you no harm.

B: Do you remember the way your father used to treat you on holidays when he made you call your relatives? He meant no harm either.

A: I see what you mean.

B: I thought you might.

A: There's no friend like an old friend.

We've all had this kind of silly conversation many times, with people we're close to and who understand why we do what we do. However, we certainly wouldn't expect to have this conversation with a machine. Computers will never understand at that level of depth simply because they won't be people—they won't have had the same experiences as people have. You cannot put inside a machine all the rules there are about all the knowledge there is in life. It's a long, endless, hopeless task. What, in fact, has to happen is that the machine has to grow its own experiences, it has to grow its own rules; it has to have expectations, they have to fail, and it has to modify them. It has to replace its structure for "restaurant" with ones for eating in fast-food restaurants, cafeterias, airplanes, and so on, to become further and further diversified. It has to have more and more experiences so that each one of the experiences adds to a little microworld in which it lives. It has to be able to make the same mistake of being in a 1918 frame of mind for a moment so that it can't see the 1984 world around it.

Expertise can't just be put into a machine; rather, it has to be grown by the machine itself. Because it will be grown by the machine, it will grow differently from the way it does in people. The machine will not behave exactly the way a person does, because machines won't have the kind of experiences we have. They will never be hungry. They will never be tired. They will never be wet. They won't be disappointed in their fellow machines.

Machines will, of course, understand, but not at the level of empathy, of having shared a large set of experiences with another being. They will, however, understand on the level of making sense; in fact, they already do.

How about the level called cognitive understanding? Cognitive understanding is the ability to add more to what you read. Imagine that a program sees a set of stories about airplane crashes and the circumstances and data surrounding them. What if, instead of paraphrasing, summarizing, and answering questions, it draws a new insight, a new conclusion about why the crashes may have occurred? How could we build a program smart enough to do that? One way is to have it involved within the data of that particular domain, to have it know lots of information about airplanes, to have it look at each one of the crash stories and not forget them, to have it then compare and contrast the different stories and learn something from the similarities it finds between them. That's the level of cognitive understanding, and although computer programs are not there yet, getting them there is an achievable goal. It's certainly possible that machines will be able to reflect, in the sense of being able to look at what they've done and come up with some new conclusions.

If understanding exists on a spectrum, how can we ever agree whether or not a computer can understand? What are the right tests to determine whether computers can understand at a particular level? A.M. Turing proposed a test that he argued might serve as a touchstone for artificial intelligence researchers in their efforts to model understanding by computer. (For an extended discussion of the Turing test, see Daniel Dennett's chapter in this volume.) The essence of this test, which Turing called the imitation game, was to challenge a person to distinguish between a computer program and another human being by putting questions to each via teletype. What Turing proposed is that we should try to discriminate a man from a woman solely on the basis of their answers to questions we pose, and then replace one by a computer and try to discriminate the computer from the human in the same way. It's not clear that you could tell the difference between a man and a woman in this setup, but it seems clear that men and women have a difficult time understanding each other. Comparing them with a computer, which is completely different from either, seems far less likely to succeed.

The requirements of Turing's test are so rigorous that no program in existence today is close to succeeding, and none is likely to be for a long time to come. (Again, see Dennett's chapter on this point.) The ultimate test of whether a computer can understand ought not to be the Turing test; the Turing test is too hard. Understanding is not a unitary phenomenon, but a spectrum—a matter of degree. If we are to evaluate the progress of AI in the short term, we must be sensitive to the possibility that programs can understand at a somewhat lower level than we normally associate with humans. The way to determine the degree of understanding is a test of computer understanding called the explanation game. AI programs should be judged by the extent to which they can explain the decisions they make and by the form these explanations take. We should be able to ask a question of a machine and have it explain why it came to a conclusion and what it imagines the consequences of its decisions will be.

A program's ability to explain its actions at a given level can give insight into the extent to which the program can be said to understand. As the previous examples illustrate, people are constantly concerned with making many types of explanations: There are coherency explanations, in which you try to explain how things fit together. This type of explanation relies upon a store of knowledge to draw inferences that create connectivity in a text, scene, or plan. There are failure explanations, in which you try to explain why a particular expectation about the world failed. This type of explanation enables people to learn; by comparing experiences that differed from expectations in the same way they can create a new set of expectations that capture the generalizations created by similar failures with similar explanations. And there are contributory explanations, in which we are seeking an understanding of the reasons behind an action that someone takes. These are explanations of what might be a motivation, in which we construct a new invention of what might make sense.

The first critical role of explanation is simply the tying together of events in such a way as to fill in the missing pieces, so as to make sure that a smooth chain of causality exists. If this can be done, then a system has understood at the making sense level. The second level of explanation implies a deeper level of understanding. Explaining failures implies the ability to understand by inter-relating a set of events in one's personal experiences, since failures are by definition violations of expectations derived from one's own experience. Explaining at this level is the basis of learning, and thus the basis of a system that can be surprised and surprising. The cognitive understanding level is thus our current goal in developing programs that are, in a limited sense, creative. The third level, complete empathy, has connected with it the level of explanation called contributory explanation. Getting a program to contemplate the possible motivations and rationale for behavior in the sophisticated sense of a psychiatrist would be an impressive demonstration of this understanding.

The real intent of AI is to find out what intelligence is all about. What makes a person really intelligent? Intelligence is the ability to pose questions to oneself and to answer them. A person is intelligent when he or she is insightful, capable of coming up with a new conclusion, or when he or she finds a new way of looking at the world. The only reason we expect that machines will ever be able to do that is that they have actually been doing something like it in a very mundane way. Perhaps they have shown some intelligence in just growing their knowledge about restaurants to the point where they can discover something profound about fast food.

The explanation game, then, isn't really a question of imitation. We are interested in finding out whether anybody or anything that we talk to can be coherent in its understanding and explanation, can be creative and self-referential in its understanding and explanation, and can be truly insightful in its understanding and explanation. Machines will demonstrate such capabilities. It's only a matter of time.

How should you understand computers and artificial intelligence? Computers are not something you should feel obligated to understand any more than you feel obligated to understand your automobile. They are something you should be able to use—if the people in AI do their jobs well. What people need to understand about artificial intelligence is not what great gizmos are on the horizon, not what kinds of strange machines we can find tomorrow in our backyards. What people need to understand is that artificial intelligence is modern-day epistemology. It's a new quest to find out more about ourselves and how we know.

DISCUSSION

Q: *Give specific suggestions, please, for encouraging and stimulating learning in preschool-age children.*

A: As a matter of fact, I have a company that produces educational software. The reason I think this is worth mentioning —in fact, the reason I'm doing it—is that if you think about the issues of intelligence and artificial intelligence, you realize that one thing intelligence is about is the ability to explain ourselves to ourselves, to reflect, to ask the right questions at the right time.

It's possible to take advantage of the personal computers all over the place these days. Right now they are in the schools for no good reason. To have them in the schools for a good reason, we need to devise games that teach reflectivity or creativity, or that teach the ability to explain. So what we've been doing is exactly that. We have invented games that teach reasoning ability and inferencing ability.

It's not that you need AI to build these games. You don't. But the ideas that AI generates can help you have a sense of what there is to teach. So I think that, although the current educational software is awful, it will be possible in the near future to place some products on the market that reflect the view of intelligence and reasoning that we have developed through AI research.

Q: *Do you foresee that we will ever be able to have computers that express emotion? And a related question: When computers at present generalize and achieve new insights, is this real understanding, even mundane understanding, or rather something vaguely and crudely analogous to understanding?*

A: This is a standard question that comes up. Suppose I got a computer to cry at the right moment, or laugh at the right moment, or be angry at the right moment in response to a story. It is possible to build programs that behave this way, that express the appropriate emotion at the appropriate time. I have often known people who have learned to behave that way, that is, to express the appropriate emotion at the appropriate time. Often one wonders whether they are really feeling it, and you would certainly be correct to wonder the same thing about the computer.

The issue is at what point the computer or person is "really feeling it." I don't know that a piece of hardware will ever actually feel something. But there is an important question underlying all that. If a computer program has a set of goals that it is trying to achieve, and if those goals are somehow frustrated, it might, in trying to reorganize its information, react in some way. I'm not suggesting that it would react angrily or happily, just that it would react or attempt to reorganize in some way, perhaps to learn from the negative experience.

To that extent I think computers could feel and express emotions. They wouldn't have the kinds of emotions that we feel and express, because they wouldn't be living, breathing organisms. Our emotions have other than pure cognitive forms. They have bodily forms. Computers, being basically minds, will have only cognitive forms of emotions, but they will be able, in principle, to react to the frustration of their goals or to success by learning. That is the level of emotion that is important for them.

With respect to the related issue of "real understanding," I think it is very hard to assess when another human being has "really understood" something. When I speak to a group or to a class, I see all those faces out there, and I have no idea whether they are understanding me or not. It's a safe bet that some are and some aren't. But I assume they are understanding me, more or less, because they all look like people, more or less. If one of them turned out to be a machine, unbeknownst to me, I would not make the same assumption. I, because I'm a human being, would assume that a machine could not "really understand" me. But that's unfair. That's a very human-chauvinistic view of life. I do believe that machines will understand and are understanding to a certain extent. Whether they're understanding in a way or to an extent that makes me feel "really understood"—that is another issue. I would have to spend a lot of time with someone, individually, to be able to feel that he or she "really understood" me at the level of complete empathy.

In other words, "real understanding" is defined very subjectively. There will be those of us who never want to say that computers can do it: "Nobody understands me." In fact, there is a range of levels and kinds of understanding. Computers, in some respects, will get pretty close to what people do, but you probably wouldn't want to marry one.

Q: *If a particular instance of expectation failure must be understood at a higher level of generalization in order to match it up with a new experience, just what is learned when the two instances (the one in memory and the new one) are compared? It seems that the higher level generalization must have already occurred in order for the "matchup" to take place.*

A: If I wasn't clear on that, it's a good point to clear up. What happens is that, when you have an expectation that fails, you remember it. I have collected many cases in which people remember an incident for up to thirty years. It lies around looking for something comparable to happen.

Take the steak-and-haircut example. What you are trying to do is to see whether the generalization you made in the case of the haircut—namely, that someone didn't want to cut your hair that extreme—has any relationship to a broader reality. Finding a similar case allows you to "scope" the generalization. Finding something similar—the case of the steak—allows you to confirm what kinds of parameters are appropriate to generalize over. So the parameters on the people are "people performing services," and the parameters on their actions are "things that are easily within their ability to do." The new case verifies for you a hypothesis you've been carrying around, perhaps unconsciously, for thirty years. (Sometimes it's only a week.) In some sense, this hypothesis is in memory, but it's waiting for verification.

We tend to learn, I argue, from two instances, not one.

Q: *Do you agree or disagree that a chess-playing computer will never beat Bobby Fischer?*

A: The whole idea of the development of a chess-playing computer has been very interesting. It has an interesting history. In the early days, it was a case of finding something smart, something that smart people do. Then if a computer could do it, you could claim that the computer was smart. So let's work on it.

Later it evolved into a challenge in its own right. That is, anything goes—a brute force approach that actually succeeded in making chess-playing programs that could beat most humans but that also destroyed any relation between what the program was doing and what a human chess player would do. The effect was to abandon the argument that chess playing was a good test of intelligence, since you could accomplish fairly good results with very low levels of intelligence.

Later on, especially under the direction of Professor Simon, we returned to much more intelligent approaches to the problem of chess playing. We began to learn about the kind of expertise a chess master might have, and we began to model that kind of knowledge in computer programs. But I think there is a fourth stage that we haven't yet reached, and that is deriving new strategies from first principles so that the computer itself could be innovative in its own approach to the game. The ultimate criterion for expertise in any area, whether chess or football or dance, is the ability to create something new.

We can build a chess-playing program by putting in all the strategic and tactical rules that a grand master might use. But the best and most interesting approach is to build a program that behaves the way Bobby Fischer behaved right from the start; namely, he played a lot of chess. He reasoned about playing chess. He improved upon old tactics. He invented things by himself that may have been invented by others as well, but the fact that he learned by inventing them for himself allowed him to go on and invent really new things.

Ultimately, creativity is the issue in AI, and we have only begun to look at that problem. I have a few projects like that in my lab. I actually have a chess-playing project, in which someone is trying to have a program play against other programs and learn how to play better chess by doing that. I have a football-coaching program, which is trying to invent new football plays. I have a cooking program, which is trying to invent new recipes. In each case, these programs invent things, and then they find out that these things didn't work so well—expectation failures—and they go back and remember various expectation failures from before and make generalizations and invent something new. Ultimately, I think this is the problem we'll have to solve. I've just started working on it, and I don't know how many others are working on it, but we're a long way from the solution.

Q: *Are there any serious ethical questions that are raised by cognitive science research?*

A: I think there are some interesting questions here. People seem to be concerned about the demystification of the human mind. Some people seem to think the less we know, the better off we are. I find that hard to understand. I think we'd be better off if we knew more.

But there *is* a real fear that people should have. It isn't that computers are going to take over. It isn't a fear of artificial intelligence at all. It's a fear that stems from the overcomputerization of our society, which manifests itself in the ability of the government to have tremendous access to every aspect of your personal life. That is a fear that is becoming more and more a reality.

Imagine that Hitler had had better computers than he had, and imagine that he wanted to know everyone who had bought a copy of a certain book. It isn't impossible to do that sort of thing in today's world. It isn't hard at all. The bookstores keep numbered inventories of books; you pay by credit card; a couple more digits in the file, and anyone could know who's buying what books.

We're not far at all from the kind of computerized society that ought to be feared. It has nothing whatever to do with artificial intelligence. It has to do with this sort of unrestricted access to information about our personal transactions.

SUGGESTED FURTHER READING

R. C. Schank and R. P. Abelson. *Scripts, Plans, Goals and Understanding: An Inquiry into Human Knowledge Structures.* (Hillsdale, N.J.: Lawrence Erlbaum Associates, 1977).

R. C. Schank and C. Riesbeck. *Inside Computer Understanding: Five Programs Plus Miniatures* (Hillsdale, N.J.: Lawrence Erlbaum Associates, 1981).

R. C. Schank. *Dynamic Memory: A Theory of Learning in Computers and People* (New York: Cambridge University Press, 1982).

R. C. Schank. *The Cognitive Computer: On Language, Learning, and Artificial Intelligence* (Reading, MA: Addison-Wesley, 1984).

4. Some Computer Models of Human Learning

HERBERT A. SIMON

I chose the title of my contribution, "Some Computer Models of Human Learning," because I think that in many ways concrete examples are the best teachers of what cognitive science and that strange area of inquiry called artificial intelligence are all about. But before I get on to my examples I need to give an introduction and place my own remarks in the context of the other chapters of this book.

One of the things that is very evident is that an area as complex as cognitive science can be investigated at many levels. In the work of Professors Edelman and Milner, we see the investigation beginning at the level of the biological brain—at the level of tissues and cells. In the work of Roger Schank we see the investigation beginning from the top down—beginning with the analysis of complex human behaviors and, in particular, verbal behaviors using natural language.

I don't think we should be surprised that there is more than one direction of approach or even more than one level of theory. The idea that we can take complex behaviors like thinking, problem solving, use of language, or understanding, and in one step of reduction explain them in terms of chemical and electrical events in neurons seems rather extravagant, rather ambitious. Instead, this field is following the example of many other natural science fields by constructing successive levels of explanation, in which the task of scientists is to reduce phenomena at one level of complexity to explanation in terms of concepts introduced at the next level down.

Here, we are in good company with the other sciences. Nobody supposes that biology can't advance until we have a complete understanding of quarks. Nobody even supposes that solid state physics can't advance until we have a full understanding of quarks. And that, of course, is fortunate. It is fortunate that science can sometimes be hung from skyhooks, because the foundations underground are often mysterious and shifting. Science often builds from both directions, from the top down and from the bottom up.

I think each of the six of us has a slightly different map of the territory, and you can take all these maps home and have an atlas. But in my map of the territory there are very definitely at least two levels—the neuron level, at which very exciting work is going on, and the information-processing level, which I hope to persuade you is equally exciting.

Just one short word on terminology. By information processing I do not mean exactly what Professor Edelman means. He was using it as a label for a particular approach within a somewhat larger category than I will be concerned with; when I talk about the neuron level and the information-processing level, I am not making the same contrast that he does between what he calls information processing and the population approach to the field.

In the last twenty-five years, it has been discovered that computers can do something besides number crunching, that they are quite general symbol-processing devices. This discovery has been exploited in at least two ways. One is in the direction called artificial intelligence, which can be very roughly defined as finding as many ways as you can to get computers to do clever things for practical reasons, or just because it's fun, or a little of both. (More exactly, performance of a computer may be called artificially intelligent if the corresponding performance of a human being would be called intelligent.) But another direction that is more often nowadays labeled cognitive science, and with which I think we're more concerned here, is the direction of using the computer to understand the nature of intelligence, the nature of mind, including the nature of the human mind. This is really the old problem of mind and body—what it is that enables a biological organ like the human brain to think.

Another distinction that will be rather important in my discussion is the distinction between systems, whether they be computers or human beings, that *perform* intelligent tasks (they play chess or they make medical diagnoses or they solve problems) and systems that *learn* to perform tasks. Because there's certainly one important difference we know between computers and human beings: in order for human beings to be able to do anything, except the limited range of things that is evidently built in, we have to learn. And since nobody knows our programming language, the internal programming language, the only way we can learn is by being exposed to experiences and to symbols from outside and, somehow or other, transforming those stimuli in such a way that the internal state of the system is changed and we're able to do new things.

What we call learning is a very impressive process if you look at its cumulative effects over a lifetime, or even over a childhood. A large number of us are still in school at age twenty, after having started the formal learning process at age six and the informal process at the time we drew our first breath; something must be wrong if it has taken us all these years to get where we are. On one hand, it's very impressive that learning can be done at all, and on the other hand, it is sometimes painfully slow. With a computer, however, you can open the lid of the box and put things in—if you know what to put in. And so computers, on some dimensions at least, can become intelligent instantaneously. They can become pretty good chess players instantaneously. Human beings probably could not reach the levels of the best programs today in less than five years of devotion to the game of chess, and most of us might never reach those levels, even if we played weekend chess all our lives.

My focus will be on learning, but if we look at the strategy of research in cognitive science over the past twenty-five years, we will see that it has been initially to try to understand human performance—first, to try to understand how it is that a human being is able to solve a problem. Having understood something about that, researchers are then beginning to go back and ask whether we can conceive of mechanisms, of processes, that could be implemented in something like a brain and that can be implemented in a computer. Can we conceive of processes that could arrive at this state of performance—that could, in fact, learn and not simply be programmed? I will try to give examples of such processes.

THE PHYSICAL SYMBOL SYSTEM HYPOTHESIS

What I will say proceeds from a hypothesis rather pretentiously called the physical symbol system hypothesis. (Unless you have a formidable name for a hypothesis, nobody will pay any attention to it, so we will continue to call this one the physical symbol system hypothesis.) By a physical symbol system I simply mean some kind of device that can deal with patterns, where a pattern is any arrangement of things. There's the pattern of a human face, which allows us to recognize it. There's a rather symmetrical pattern of rafters that hold up the roof of a house. So by *pattern* I simply mean some kind of arrangement that we can learn to discriminate from other and different arrangements, or that we can learn to compare with similar arrangements, just as we can see the regularity of the steps in a staircase or the rafters in a house.

What can we do with patterns? For one thing, both human beings and also, it turns out, computers, can read patterns; that is, patterns can be ingested from some external sensory source. They can be *written*—that is, patterns can be created in the environment by the system itself. They can be *stored* in what we call memory; they can be kept around for a long time, more or less accurately and presumably with more or less reliability. Patterns can be put in relation to each other—in classical psychological terminology, they can be *associated,* and similarly, in nonhuman pattern devices, we can build up relations so that one pattern points to another pattern in the system. As I've already suggested, patterns can be *compared;* I can compare my two hands, match them by putting together my fingertips, and see that they are more or less similar instances of the same pattern—the human hand. You can have strict tests of comparison or looser tests. The test I applied to my hands didn't notice that one was a left hand and one was a right hand.

The physical symbol system hypothesis is this: The necessary and sufficient condition that a system be capable of behaving intelligently is that it be a physical symbol system. The necessary and sufficient condition that a system be able to solve problems, to think, to use language, to understand, is that it be able to read symbols (that is, sense them), to write symbols, to set up structures of related symbols, to store those structures in memory, to compare symbols to see whether they're the same or different, and to behave differentially on the basis of whether those symbols are, in fact, the same or different.

There are several corollaries to the physical symbol system hypothesis. The first corollary is that if the hypothesis is true, it follows that computers can be made to behave intelligently. We know that computers are physical symbol systems—we can find that out by opening the box, so to speak. They have all the simple capabilities that I have mentioned—reading and writing, and so on. So if the hypothesis is true, computers can be made to be intelligent.

The second corollary is that if the hypothesis is true, if this is the necessary condition for intelligence, then human beings must be at least physical symbol systems, because human beings are capable of behaving intelligently. I haven't defined intelligence, by the way. I simply am using it in its commonsense meaning. We all know how we judge our friends to be intelligent, but we also have all sorts of formal tests, which generally consist of giving someone a task and seeing how successfully that task is handled. Intelligence is no unitary thing, because people can be very intelligent along some dimensions and very unintelligent along others. That is all I mean by intelligence, and when I talk about a computer being intelligent, I'm going to apply to it the same kinds of tests I will apply to the human being. I will judge its intelligence by the range and kinds of tasks that it can perform that, if performed by a human, we would say required intelligence. (See Professor Dennett's chapter for a detailed discussion of this point.)

So that's the hypothesis—that human beings must be physical symbol systems and that computers can be programmed to behave intelligently. No one needs to accept the hypothesis or reject it in any hurry; there's plenty of time to consider it. It's an empirical hypothesis: We test it by looking at empirical facts; we test it by running experiments. For example, if we want to know whether a computer is intelligent in being able to perform a certain kind of task, we can try to write a program that will enable the computer to perform tasks of that class, and as wide a class as possible.

If we want to test the hypothesis that people, in fact, are intelligent because they behave as physical symbol systems—because they have these properties of manipulating symbols in their brains

—it's a little bit more complicated. The usual strategy of testing that's been adopted in cognitive science in the past twenty-five years is something like this: One writes a computer program, since we already know that the computer is a physical symbol system. One tries to write a program that can perform some intelligent task that we might ask a human to perform, and perform it in a demonstrably human way—not fly as an airplane flies, but fly as a bird flies (if we want to understand birds); not play chess by trying millions of combinations, which a computer can do (and the best programs do), but play chess by looking very selectively at the important features of the board, which we know to be the way a skillful human being plays chess. In sum, we try to describe symbol-manipulating processes (the program) that can simulate closely, and account for, intelligent human performance of the same tasks.

Such a computer program is a theory of human behavior. We test the theory by letting it generate its consequences. In this case, we let the theory, the computer program, generate a stream of behavior. We let it make a move in chess, or we let it solve an algebra problem. And we see whether, step by step, it seems to follow the same kinds of backwaters that a human being does in solving the same problems.

This kind of evidence has been accumulating about a limited range of human tasks for about twenty-five years. We still are far from testing the hypothesis over the whole range of things that human beings do and call intelligent. Professor Schank, in the third chapter of this volume, calls to our attention some of the difficulties in simulating, by computer, human behavior in areas like everyday use of language. There are indeed such difficulties, and there's plenty of research to be done in continuing to test this hypothesis. There will be work for all who are motivated to join this game, work for several generations, I'm sure.

As I have said, the early activity in this field was mostly directed to performance—to getting computers to play chess, make medical diagnoses, solve the Tower of Hanoi problem, get the missionaries and cannibals across the river, or whatever your favorite puzzle happens to be. But in recent years progress toward understanding intelligent performance in more complex tasks has encouraged strong renewal of research in cognitive science about learning.

That research has produced a number of computer systems that are capable of learning, some of them in a quite humanoid manner, others in manners that may or may not bear any close relation to human learning. I have chosen three of those systems to discuss, examples that I'm especially familiar with. They are not in any sense a random or even a representative sample of work in this field.

ROTE VERBAL LEARNING

For the first fifty years or so of the history of psychology, from the time of Ebbinghaus and Wundt in Germany, psychologists were fascinated with how people did verbal learning. In those days, schoolchildren still had to learn lots of poetry and lots of foreign language vocabulary. I am told that children don't memorize nearly as many things in school now as they did in days gone by, and I don't know quite what to think of that. I guess it's a good thing.

At any rate, psychologists became preoccupied with these kinds of verbal learning processes—even the rote learning processes that constituted a large part of school activity. And there's a vast body of psychological literature that describes what human beings do when they're faced with a verbal learning task. Ebbinghaus wanted to do this really scientifically; he wanted to control variables, so he invented something called nonsense syllables that don't have any meaning, and he did most of his experiments with them. But we won't get into nonsense (that kind at least); we'll talk about learning in general.

There exists, and has, in fact, existed for twenty-five years, a computer program known as EPAM, which stands for Elementary Perceiver and Memorizer. EPAM is capable of learning—learning either a series of items, the way we learned the alphabet, or learning associations between pairs of items, the way we might learn foreign language vocabulary. There's no claim that EPAM understands semantically the things that it learns; EPAM is an attempt to model the human learning process when humans are learning things more or less by rote.

Today we can explain most of the main phenomena that were

discovered in the verbal learning laboratories of psychologists. We can explain those phenomena with the EPAM program, in the sense that if you give EPAM the same materials that were given to the human learners, it will produce the same kinds of phenomena. For example, it has been demonstrated many times that syllables consisting of three unrelated letters, real nonsense syllables, take about three times as long to learn as simple one-syllable meaningful words. Without trying to explain here how EPAM does it, here's a program that predicts, in fact, that English words will be learned about three times faster than three-letter nonsense syllables.

Similarity or dissimilarity between items that are being learned also affects learning—in some cases it facilitates it, and in some cases it interferes with it. EPAM can predict the major effects along those dimensions, also. The mechanisms within EPAM that cause it to model the human behavior so closely constitute a plausible theory of the processes of human verbal learning.

SHORT-TERM MEMORY, RECOGNITION, AND INTUITION

Out of the research on the EPAM model and similar models, combined with laboratory research using human subjects, two important ideas began to emerge. One of them was around before EPAM—introduced by George Miller in 1956. This idea was that it is terribly important in human performance to have a focus of attention, otherwise known as a short-term memory. Everything we pay attention to, everything we do that requires some modicum of attention, has to be squeezed through the bottleneck of our short-term memory. When we add a column of figures, those figures, one by one as well as the running total, have to be in short-term memory.

Short-term memory is an extremely narrow bottleneck, and it turns out to be one of the most important features of the architecture of the human thinking system in determining the rate at which we can think and the way in which information has to be organized so that we can carry out complex sequences of thoughts. Today, we speak of the short-term memory as though it were a little box with no more than six or seven little compartments in it in which are stored something like a half-dozen familiar items, where a familiar item might be anything you have become acquainted with. For college-educated people, familiar items might be any one of the fifty thousand English words in their vocabulary. (This quantity has been estimated, and it is of that order of magnitude. It may actually be twice that number, but we won't quibble about factors of two here.)

If I give you a list of six words, you can hold them in memory long enough to repeat them back to me. But watch out if I give you nine. You're going to be in trouble. There is a vast body of experimental evidence that is compatible with the model of a limited short-term memory and that is predictable by the model. We think today that the structure of the short-term memory has a very great deal to do with the way in which knowledge is stored in the mind of an expert. We believe that a great deal of what the expert is able to do, he or she is able to do because of an ability to recognize cues in a familiar situation—recognize cues in any situation within the domain of expertness—and having recognized those cues, to use them to access relevant information in long-term memory.

It doesn't surprise you that when you see the face of a familiar friend you immediately recognize it. Moreover, though not all of us are good at this, you can probably retrieve from long-term memory the name of the friend, or if not the name, a lot of facts about the friend. This process of recognition followed by retrieval from long-term memory underlies most human expertise. We even have estimates today of how many chunks—the same familiar little chunks you store in a short-term memory—it requires to make an expert. Again, the answer comes out, in order of magnitude, to be around fifty thousand. For example, a chess grandmaster can recognize fifty thousand or more different kinds of features and patterns of pieces that are likely to occur on a chess board during a game.

Just to provide you with a sample of the kinds of experimental evidence that buttress hypotheses like this, I'll give a short description of a classical chess experiment. You take a chess board, eight by eight squares, and arrange on it, at, maybe, the twentieth move, the pieces from a well-played game—a game that's well played but unfamiliar to the subjects in the experiment. You display this position to your subjects for five to ten seconds and then withdraw it;

then you ask them to reproduce the chessboard. If a subject is a master or a grand master, the pieces will be replaced almost perfectly, with better than 90 percent accuracy, even though there are twenty-three pieces, on average, on such a board. If the player is something less than a master or an expert, at least, he or she will be lucky to get six pieces back on the board correctly. Oh, you will say, you need special kinds of eyes, special kinds of visual imagery, to be a chess master or grand master.

But, let's take the next step in the experiment. We simply take the same pieces and arrange them at random on the board and expose them to the subjects for five to ten seconds. Now the ordinary chess player replaces about six pieces on the board just as before—and the master or the grand master replaces about six pieces on the board. It has nothing to do with the eyes, but a great deal to do with how many hours have been spent in staring at chess boards—misspent youth you might say—how many patterns have become familiar and have been stored away in long-term memory, associated with information about what to do when such a pattern is seen on the board. And so we observe the expert in every field of expertise, not only recognizing familiar friends in the situations he or she sees, but also recalling all sorts of information about these friends—the doctor looking at your spots and saying, "Oh yes, that's measles"—and forming an immediate hypothesis (subject to revision) about what might be going on. And so we think today that this kind of performance—this kind of expert intuition, if you want to call it that, or insight—can be given a perfectly reasonable explanation in information-processing terms, in terms of recognition processes.

SOLVING ALGEBRAIC EQUATIONS

Let us go on to another kind of learning, because we all know that rote learning really isn't a very good thing except for special purposes. Rote learning is great to get through the Friday quiz, but by Monday it seems all to have evaporated again. We really want to talk about learning with understanding. What does it mean to understand what we've learned? Roger Schank has pointed out that the word *understanding* may mean many different things, and I'm only going to touch on one or two of them.

Each of us has probably had occasion with greater or lesser pleasure to learn to do algebra, at least simple algebra. We learned to solve equations. The teacher would write on the board:

$$3x + 4 = x + 10$$

Probably you still remember what to do about such an equation and can solve it in a moment or two. But suppose your child said, "I'm having trouble with my algebra tonight. Will you help me?" Probably few of us would have immediately on the tip of our tongue a clear *explanation* of exactly how the trick was done. Maybe you can do it yourself, but do you know what you are doing while you are doing it? There's been a good deal of study now of how people solve simple algebraic equations—a simple skill, but typical of the skills that we use in school, particularly but not exclusively in science.

In the first version, I won't even refer to algebra. I am in a certain situation, standing in front of a podium. I need to be in a different situation; eventually I'm going to have to walk down and leave. Now, I have to ask what the difference is in position or in place. What do I know? What knowledge do I have that tells me how to reduce such differences? Well, there are bicycles, there are taxis, there's something called shank's mare. Bicycles and taxis aren't very appropriate here, it would be a little hard getting them down the stairway, it might be hard getting them into the hall; but I always do have my legs. And so we've solved this very simple problem. When the time comes, I'm going to walk down—a very deep solution. It takes babies a year or so before they're able to do that.

The thing I've been describing with this stupidly simple example is something called means-ends analysis. I'm here, my goal is to be there; I detect a difference between where I am and the goal; I use that as a cue to reach into memory to see whether I have any experience in reducing differences of that kind. Yes, there is such a means of reducing differences, and I apply it. I am now closer to my goal, maybe I'm at the head of the stairs. Now I have to have a new difference-reducing means called walking down stairs—and so on.

How do we do algebra by means-ends analysis? Very simply. I have an expression like $3x + 4 = x + 10$; what do I want? Well,

I'll have a solution if I have an *x* followed by an equals sign, followed by a number *x = n*. Of course, it has to be the right number. It doesn't pay off if you just write down any number; that would make the problem too easy. I need an *x,* an equals sign, and a number.

How do I change an expression like the one I have into one that consists of just $x = n$? Well, we do have all kinds of operations. We're allowed, without altering the value of *x*, to subtract a term, as long as we subtract it from both sides of the equation. We're allowed to add a term as long as we add it to both sides. We may multiply both sides by the same term and divide both sides by the same term (but we must watch out for zeros). That's about all we're allowed to do, isn't it? Those are the only actions. We can add, subtract, multiply, and divide the same quantity on both sides of the equation.

If I have an equation that does not have only *x*'s on the right side and numbers on the left, and I want to reduce it to an equation with just an *x,* an equals sign, and a number, I must get rid of some of those differences. Let's subtract away the numbers on the left side, which I don't want in the final result; then let's subtract away the *x* on the right side, which I don't want in the final result. If you've worked this out, you will find you have a 2*x* on the left side by now, so let's divide by two, and we will end up with an *x* and an equals sign, and a three, assuming I did it right. An *x,* an equals sign, and a three. We can check whether I did it right by sticking the answer back into the equation. The whole process looks like this:

$$3x + 4 = x + 10$$
$$3x = x + 6$$
$$2x = 6$$
$$x = 3$$
$$3 \times 3 + 4 = 3 + 10 = 13$$

Today we know how to describe a system that proceeds in this way in terms of computer programs, and when we do describe the processes that enable a person to solve this equation, they look very much like the processes that allow the physician to be an expert diagnostician, and that allow the chess player to be a grand master. In the case of the physician, "If you see those spots, guess that it might be measles, and suggest the following tests." If you're the chess player, "If you see that open file, consider putting a rook on it. Don't do it in a hurry, think about it awhile, but consider putting a rook on it." If you're solving algebra problems: "If the equation has a number on the left-hand side, consider subtracting that number from both sides."

If you've studied stimulus response psychology, behaviorist psychology, you can think of such a procedure as a stimulus followed by a response. If you've studied computer science, instead, you can think of it as something that nowadays we call a production—a condition or cue, followed by an action.

If condition C is satisfied, then take action A. Our hypothesis is that most human skill is embodied in the brain in the form of productions, a perceptual capability of responding to a cue followed by retrieval of information about the action to take.

The person who does this algebra problem doesn't have to have fifty thousand chunks of information. But to do algebra problems of this degree of difficulty—learned from about one week's work in the algebra course—you need a set of just four productions. I've already sketched them for you. Any system, including a computer or a human brain, can solve simple equations if it has a way of storing and applying the following set of procedures:

If there's a number on the left, subtract it from both sides.
If there's an x on the right, subtract that from both sides.
If there's a number multiplying x on the left and the number isn't one, divide both sides by it.
If you have an expression that looks like $x = n$, halt and check.

Four productions will do a whole range of these algebra problems.

I do not mean that you can learn to do algebra by memorizing those four rules. When I say those rules have to reside in the brain in order for you to do algebra, I mean that there has to be present the perceptual skill of recognizing the cues (the "if" conditions) and for accessing in memory the knowledge of what actions to take (the right-hand sides of the productions). For most of us, at least those of us who have continued to use our algebraic skills, those four productions are so well stored that they no longer require much conscious attention for their application. I won't go into the question of consciousness, but frequent repetition automates and

makes subconscious the application of a great many of these productions, so that a simple recognition occurs and an action follows
it. Such "intuitive" responses are characteristic of expert behavior
in algebra.

LEARNING ALGEBRA

If I have correctly or even partially correctly characterized the way
some skills are held inside the human skull, then it becomes an
interesting question as to how learning of these skills takes place.
How might a person acquire such production systems? Again, the
computer comes to our aid, because today we know how to program so-called adaptive production systems. There's nothing very
formidable about an adaptive production system; it is simply a set
of productions that includes a subset capable of constructing or
generating new symbol structures in the form of productions.
After all, productions must be stored in the brain in whatever
symbolic language the brain is using, and what an adaptive production system does is to create new symbol structures, new productions, of exactly the same kind and put them into the system.
Once they are in the system, they are operative and can run along
with all the others that are there already.

How might that work with the algebra example? Suppose we
have a clever student—and this idea was initially suggested by
watching clever students—who encounters this chapter of the algebra textbook for the first time. One thing the student might do
is to read it through very thoroughly. This is very unlikely. Another
thing a clever student might do is page through and see if there
are some worked-out examples. Surely there will be some. Then
the student will study a worked-out example very carefully, study
it in the sense of—well, what makes it work? What makes it tick?
After a little while that clever student may be able to solve simple
linear equations. We see that happening all the time with our
clever students in school. They do a lot of their learning from
worked-out examples, sometimes worked-out examples in the
classroom on the blackboard, very often worked-out examples in
the textbook.

What is going on there? You see, all the information that is
needed to construct the production system for solving such prob-

lems is present in the textbook example. The student can compare successive lines of the solution, can see what changes have been made, and, by comparing those changes to the final result, $x = n$, can see the motivation for the changes, can see the gradual reduction of differences between the original expression and the final expression.

Of course, I'm waving my hands, which in computer language means I'm passing over all the difficult issues; but there are running programs today that do this, essentially by using means-ends analysis, but using it in a questioning mode: "Such and such an action was taken, the person moved over there. Why?" Let's compare the situation with the goal that was being aimed at. Let's now define a difference in terms of how we were brought nearer to that goal by that action. Let's associate that difference with the action that was taken. Now we have a new production. We stuff it into the system. It's ready to go the next time a similar situation is encountered.

Can this work with human beings? Can you construct teaching material on this basis? In fact, it has been done; the example I'm going to give now is from an experiment in which children were presented the tasks of factoring quadratic expressions. The reason we didn't experiment with solving equations, but with factoring of quadratic expressions instead, had to do with the particular point in the school year when we were ready to do the experiment. The students had already done equations, and they were just coming on to factoring. We constructed a set of written materials of only three or four pages and consisting wholly of worked-out examples and problems for the students to work. The worked-out examples were carefully designed to introduce the differences between the present situation and the goal one by one. We presented these to classes of students. (We happen to have done this in China, but I think it will work just as well with American students. We'll find out in the coming year.) Within twenty minutes, 90 percent of the students in those classes were factoring quadratics. I don't know whether you think that's a great thing or whether you learned that very easily when you studied algebra, but usually about two days of the algebra curriculum is devoted to learning to factor quadratics.

I don't want to make too much of a single experiment that will certainly need to be repeated many times and will need to be compared with other methods of teaching. The point is that, not only can you build for a computer an adaptive production system that will teach itself to solve equations in algebra or to factor quadratics by looking at worked-out examples, but you also can use this method for teaching human children. It appears, at first blush at least, to be a reasonably effective method.

The first comment we got from the teacher of the first class in which we ran such an experiment was, "And you didn't say a word to them." He evidently had the faith, which all us college professors hold, that the way to spread the germs of knowledge is by spraying words on our audiences. It seemed to him a little magical that the whole thing could be brought off without words. Of course, there *were* written words, or at least written equations, in the teaching materials.

The other point of this example is that cognitive science has now reached a point in its development at which it is no longer dealing just with toy tasks. It is no longer just dealing with getting missionaries and cannibals across the river. It is dealing with school level tasks. For that reason, if enough excitement can be generated about this area of research (and I can't imagine why it won't generate excitement), and if enough bright people will come into this area, I think it can be brought into real relevance to the educational process within a reasonable number of years. I think that's an important task for us in the years ahead.

DISCOVERY: EXTRACTING LAWS FROM DATA

Let me turn to a quite different example. As we all know, computers can only do what you tell them to do. Even these systems I've been describing were only doing what we told them to do. An adaptive production system was simply learning from examples because we told it to learn from examples. If you think about it that way, you see that you can tell computers to do quite general things. How general? How vague can the specification be?

The way to get some hint about how human beings attack vague problems—like many of the problems we deal with in everyday life and many of the problems we deal with in science—is to see whether we can, in fact, give a computer more general tasks. I suppose we would think that the task of discovering laws by seeing patterns in raw data might be one that would require a certain amount of independent thinking. Maybe we'd even want to use that sacred word *creativity* to apply to a human being who is able to take some data and out of these data find order and some kind of regularity or scientific law. That will be our arena of study.

The first example comes not out of science but out of intelligence tests. One standard kind of item in an intelligence test is the so-called Thurstone letter series completion task. You're given a sequence of letters, and you're asked what comes next: for example, *A B M, C D M,* what's next?—*E F M.* Now, there are some mathematicians who will say, "Anything could have been next." That's perfectly true, I could have started over again, A B M, or done anything. However, I would advise you that, if you take such a test and want to get into college, you'd better answer *E F M.*

What was involved? How did you do that? What's this mysterious process of seeing a pattern? It's not so mysterious. It's based on the elementary symbol processing procedures I mentioned at the very beginning. You saw in the sequence I read the letter *M* —you saw it twice. You compared two symbols, and they seemed the same, *A B M, C D M,* so you had an anchor point there. You could at least conjecture that perhaps an *M* would appear periodically in the sequence.

Secondly, you know about the English alphabet. You know that *B* follows *A,* that *D* follows *C,* and therefore you know that a reasonable thing to follow the *D* is an *E.* To solve the problem, you used your knowledge in memory of the alphabet, plus your knowledge in memory about identity of letters, plus your ability to recognize situations in which these simple patterns show up. When one thing follows another in orderly succession, the way the lines do on this page, you are prepared to notice that repetition, and you are prepared to notice such sequences in alphabets, in numbers, and in a few other series. In music, for example, you can notice the sequence of the diatonic and chromatic scales, the cycle of fifths —all of those elements of musical pattern that enable us to know whether we are listening to Bach or Beethoven. Our detection of patterns can be shown to be based on the ability to recognize repetition and the ability to recognize sequence.

Here we have already discovered a very simple scientific law.

We've learned that after $A\ B\ M$, $C\ D\ M$, there follows $E\ F\ M$. Let's consider laws that have had more historical interest than that particular law. Kepler looked at the heavens. It was very hard to look at the heavens in those days. They had very primitive instruments, but he and his predecessors were able to get some data about the distances of the planets from the sun and the period of time it took for each of the planets to revolve around the sun. Kepler wondered whether there was a relation. He found one, and it is called Kepler's third law.

We have today a computer program called BACON, named, of course, after Sir Francis Bacon because it believes very deeply in Francis Bacon's ideas about induction. What the program BACON does, following the advice of Sir Francis, is to look at data and try to induce patterns from those data. The first thing it looks for in data are correlations. In this case of planetary motion, it would discover that as the distance of the planet increases, the period of revolution also increases. What BACON is looking for is, of course, an invariant—some kind of invariant law hidden in the data.

If you have one variable that's increasing while another one increases, one primitive idea is to try dividing one by the other, for maybe the ratio will then be a constant. BACON does that—no luck, no constant. It gets a new quantity, P/D, period of revolution over the diameter of the orbit. But it notices that P/D is also correlated with D, the diameter of the orbit, so it tries dividing again. It gets P/D^2—still no jackpot, still no invariant. It now notices that P/D^2 and P/D vary in opposite directions; as one goes up the other goes down. Well, maybe we'll have luck. Maybe if we multiply them together, we'll get an invariant. It multiplies them together, and finds an invariant: P^2/D^3, which is Kepler's third law.

Notice that BACON is trying different functions, but notice also that it's not doing it at all in a random way. And notice that, in fact, it finds the correct function after very little trial and error. I've oversimplified a little bit, but essentially that is what it does, and it does that in less than a minute on a modern computer. Kepler took maybe ten years, but he was preoccupied with other things. His mother was being tried for witchcraft during part of that period, and life was rather complicated.

I'm not going to give a long list of examples of what BACON does, but one other example will serve to illustrate that quite understandable processes—let's call them natural processes—can be used by an information-processing system to discover natural laws.

Suppose I have two objects and a spring connecting them. If you stretch the spring and then release it, the objects will be accelerated. Suppose we can measure those accelerations. BACON will rapidly find that the ratio of acceleration of object A to that of object B will be the same no matter how much it's stretched or how little it's stretched. The ratio of accelerations will be the same: here is a little scientific law.

Take two different objects now, or object A and a third object, and again we'll find the ratio of the accelerations is constant, but a different constant. Now under circumstances in which BACON finds a law that expresses a relation between two objects, BACON will try to attribute a property to each object such that the properties will explain the behavior of the objects. In this case BACON will assign a number M_A to object A and then it will find that M_A multiplied by the acceleration of object A, plus M_B multiplied by the acceleration of object B is always zero, which is an expression of the law of conservation of momentum.

$$M_A a_A + M_B a_B = 0$$

Notice that BACON did two things here. First, it introduced new concepts. Nobody told it about properties of the two objects. It introduced such a property—the property that we know as inertial mass. Second, by the use of the new property, it discovered a law—in this case, a very basic conservation law of physics, the conservation of momentum.

Given other kinds of data, BACON has succeeded in introducing the concept of specific heat in experiments involving mixing liquids at different temperatures, a problem that defied solution for about thirty years after the invention of the Fahrenheit thermometer. Fahrenheit and Boerhaave, Dutch chemists, got halfway, but they were stumped when it turned out that mercury was much heavier than water, and they thought it ought to absorb more heat. It was Joseph Black, the Scottish chemist, who introduced the idea of "specific heat." BACON, knowing nothing about temperature or heat, arrives, purely by induction from the data, at the concept of specific heat.

Using data on refracted light, it also introduces the concept of the index of refraction. And it can find many more concepts and laws. I won't go down the list of BACON's wonders, but I think BACON does demonstrate that one can begin to model and explain those forms of human intelligence that are usually supposed to involve genuine creativity. One can think about what processes would lead a scientist to discover a new scientific law.

Now, inferring things from data is not the only way in which scientists infer new laws. I want to make that quite clear. But we can show historically that in the case of Ohm, who invented Ohm's law of electricity, in the case of Kepler, in many other celebrated cases in the history of science, there was no particular theoretical foundation for the discovery—the discovery had to be an induction from fact because that's all there was. BACON shows how discoveries of these kinds can be made by a physical symbol system.

REPRESENTATION OF KNOWLEDGE

One other area needs mention. That is the area now usually called representation. From human psychological experimentation we have good evidence that when someone takes a problem presented in words, translates that problem into a set of equations, and then solves the equations—or when someone is given a statement in the French language and translates it into English—the process is not one of direct conversion from the code of the input language into the output language, that is, the mathematical equations, or the English. There intervenes between input stimulus and output response some kind of internal representation, some other way of holding the meaningful context of the stimulus information in the head. We usually call this intervening symbol structure a semantic representation. It serves as a mediator between the input and the output.

You don't translate from French to English—at least not if you're any good at French and English. You translate from French to the meaning of the French (the semantic representation) and from the meaning of the French into English. It sounds like a slow way around, but it's really the only fast and correct way. Similarly, suppose a physicist, or a student in high school, is given one of those problems about an 80 percent alcohol-and-water mixture that he or she wants to dilute into a 60 percent alcohol-and-water mixture. The students who are successful in solving such problems do so by means of an internal representation of the problem that precedes the writing of the equation. One of the important goals today of cognitive science and artificial intelligence is to understand the nature of these internal representations. I won't try to tell in any breadth what we know about these matters, but I will give an example of what I mean by an internal representation so you can get a feel for it.

We all talk about mental pictures. That gives philosophers great difficulty, because they tell us that if you have a mental picture, there must be a little man inside looking at the picture, and then what kind of picture does the little man have? You can get into all sorts of regressions if you allow your mind to stray in that way. So, let's ask what *mental picture* could mean. Imagine a rectangle that is exactly twice as broad as it is high. Now drop a line from the middle of the top of the rectangle to its bottom; it divides it in two, doesn't it? And the two halves are each squares. Now I want you to draw a diagonal from the northwest corner of your rectangle to the southeast corner—from Seattle to Miami. Does that line intersect the line that you drew bisecting the rectangle from top to bottom?

Now the interesting point here, of course, is not that it does intersect. How many people could use the methods of mathematics to prove that it intersects? In fact, that's a rather difficult problem in topology and geometry. Although we all instantly and clearly *see* the intersection, it's difficult to prove these two lines intersect. If you use analytical geometry to write down equations for the lines, it's just a little easier. Do you suppose that you or the homunculus in your head performed the analytic geometry? Well, maybe.

The problem of semantic representation is the problem of understanding how operations of that kind can be performed on information in the human head. And certainly, it appears to those of us, or to most of us, who are researching in this area that those operations are not the operations of deductive logic. They are simple processing operations, of a much more direct kind than logical inference. I don't have a good label for them, because there's still a lot of dispute as to how they might go on.

If I were to carry on my example of that rectangle and add other information, I could soon convince you that even if you have a picture of the rectangle, it's far short of a photograph. If I added about three more lines, you would have about as much information as you are able to keep about that rectangle. In any case, you can hold a limited amount of information, but information that somehow or other is able to generate geometric properties that are not explicitly given in the description of the picture. I didn't tell you about that intersection. I never mentioned it.

CONCLUSION

Today there are important open problems in the area of artificial intelligence with respect to how the human head stores and processes these kinds of semantic representations. Roger Schank has referred to this in other contexts, and he has raised other kinds of problems of internal representation. What does this all add up to? What conclusions should we draw from it?

I've already mentioned one. Cognitive science has progressed to the point today where we can begin to understand, not just toy examples of human intelligence at work, but also real examples, examples at the level of school and professional tasks, of intelligence at work. We can often model that intelligence by building computer simulations that track very closely the human performance and even the human errors. If we're not interested in simply modeling the human performance, we can also write computer programs that can serve as experts for us. In this way, we can augment human intelligence, and within the past three or four years the construction of such experts has become a very popular game and even a serious economic enterprise in this country.

But as far as applications are concerned, in many ways the most interesting and the most important are the possible applications to pedagogy. We have operated our institutions of learning for too many years on the word-spraying theory that I mentioned earlier —because it was the only theory we had available. Just as medicine, when it began to understand the physiology of the human body, was able to begin to achieve results in the prevention and cure of disease that it had not been able to achieve simply on the basis of folk art and skill, so, as we begin to understand what it is that a person has to learn in order to engage in an intelligent or skilled performance, we are going to be able to improve the educational process at all levels in our schools.

I think these developments have another implication or set of implications that we all sense. They really go very much to the root of the human view of our own species, of ourselves. Every so often there comes along some event in the world of ideas that forces humankind to reconsider ourselves, our whole position in the universe, and to re-evaluate our sense of worth. I think the computer is having that impact.

Copernicus came along, and we could no longer believe that our little planet was at the center of things. We're just circling around the sun, and the sun isn't even at the center of things. It's out on the wing of some galaxy, and goodness knows where that galaxy is. That was a shocking idea. But we got used to it. I don't think anybody today lies sleepless at night wondering how to get the earth back into the center of the universe, or being terribly unhappy that it isn't there.

Then came along a man named Darwin. Well, not all of us have gotten over Darwin yet, but most of us have: the great shock of learning that the human species had origins of the same kind as other species, that the mechanisms bringing about its creation were the same mechanisms that brought about the creation of other and more humble beasts. We had to give up the idea of our uniqueness after Darwin, and most of us have made our peace with him. We no longer have to be especially created in that way, in that sense, in order to feel our human worth.

Today there are people, and you've been reading one of them, who say, in the best tradition of antivitalist biology, that a human being is a natural organism, a biological organism. They say the reason we human beings can think is that we have neurons and other structures in the brain capable of supporting an information-processing system, a physical symbol system, of the kind I've been describing. This is why we can think.

It turns out that computers, with a completely different kind of "hardware" from people, are also able to support information processing, symbol processing, and therefore are also able to think. And so we are beginning to get used to the idea that there are other creatures in creation besides ourselves who are capable of intelligence. Of course we've known that all along. We know that our dog can think and our cat can think, but they only think little thoughts. We were the ones on this earth who could think the big thoughts. Now computers have come, and from time to time they're thinking some rather big thoughts, indeed. So, we undergo a third challenge to our uniqueness.

Maybe there's a solution to this if it troubles us. Maybe it is not just a solution to this specific problem but a solution in a slightly more general sense. Maybe the trouble is not that we're losing any particular sense of our uniqueness; maybe the trouble consists in considering that it is our uniqueness that defines us as human beings, our uniqueness that provides human worth in this world. Maybe the solution is to find again a way of relating ourselves to the world in which we live—not by finding a new basis for pride, for judging ourselves in some respect superior to the rest of nature; not by setting ourselves apart from nature, but by recognizing at last that we are a part of nature, and that we must learn to live at peace with nature.

DISCUSSION

Q: *Dr. Simon, I find it extremely difficult to believe that BACON introduces new concepts. Surely it introduces a symbol that the observer interprets as inertial mass, specific heat, and so forth. If we didn't already have the theoretical context, these symbols would be meaningless and uninterpreted. The computer has discovered nothing, because it could never have supplied the theory in which the terms are embedded and outside of which they lack meaning. Comment?*

A: I think I would prefer to continue to say that BACON introduces new concepts. Let's take the concept of inertial mass, which I used in my example. If one takes classical mechanics, and formalizes the conceptual apparatus that's used in classical mechanics, then at some time in that formalization, one has to introduce a symbol that corresponds to inertial mass. And if you look at the way in which that actually happens, in an axiomatization of classical mechanics, it turns out to require what the logicians call an existential quantification.

That is, if you try to state Newton's laws of motion for celestial phenomena, you'll find yourself at some point writing down a law that says, There exists a set of numbers m_n such that $m_1 a_1$ (where a is the acceleration again) plus $m_2 a_2$, and so forth, equals zero—exactly the expression that I used in my example. So, if one talks about BACON simply introducing a symbol, then I'm afraid one would have to talk about just introducing a symbol in humanly axiomatized physics, too.

The symbol takes on its meaning because of the role that it plays in the law that describes the phenomena. The symbol that BACON introduces takes on its meaning because it turns out to be associated with the fact that some bodies resist acceleration more than other bodies. And there's nothing there except the symbol and the connection between the symbol and the phenomena that are described in the law. So I really don't know what it means to say "an uninterpreted symbol," unless you would also say in exactly the same technical sense that mass in an axiomatization of classical mechanics is an uninterpreted symbol.

Q: *Dr. Simon, Descartes said that science has the perspective of studying the uniquely simple problems in material nature. Repetitive processes yield nicely to science and math. However, unique processes, heroism, love, mercy, diverge from this adaptive model, from repetitive processes. They also seem rather nonmaterial. How do you relate these characteristics to perception of the nonuniqueness of human beings in nature?*

A: Of course, I relied on the fact that this conference is dealing with cognitive science, not with human beings in general, and I tried to be very careful in introducing physical symbol systems to say that a human being is *at least* a physical symbol system. Now the human brain resides in the head, and the head, of course, is connected with the body, and the connection is thought to be important—important enough so that most people are reluctant to have the two separated from each other.

In order to introduce any of the concepts of human motivation and affect, we would have to have a much more elaborate and comprehensive theory than any of us are discussing or proposing at this conference. We would have to have a theory, at the very least, if we consider the biological aspects of it, that had an autonomic nervous system, which would tell us when we were hungry, which would send us all sorts of stimuli other than the stimuli we get through our external senses. And I think Roger Schank pointed out very effectively that one of the reasons that it's hard to talk about things like love or heroism in connection with a computer is that a computer has none of those connections with the body, and that a computer, or at least computers of our generation, have almost none of the experiences that human beings store away and that are relevant to those aspects of our lives. That is the way I would prefer to describe the distinction, and I would personally prefer, I guess, not to take the processes you mentioned out of the realm of biology, but they certainly are outside the realm of current cognitive science.

Q: *On what do you base the assumption that the processes used to solve well-structured problems are the same as those that are used to solve ill-structured problems? Aren't there metaprocesses of problem epistemology that must be worked out in ill-structured problems?*

A: Well, of course, we don't know that the processes I've described would work for ill-structured problems. We'll learn the answer as we press further and further into the domain of ill-structured problems. It's an interesting working hypothesis that the processes are the same. Cognitive science, like all sciences, has started by dealing with the problems it thought it could deal with. It started with tasks like puzzles and has moved on to tasks like physics and algebra and geometry, and at each step, as we move into problems that are less well defined, the question has to be re-asked: Will the same set of processes work in this domain as worked in the previous domain? That is an empirical question. I've had some speculations about how we can extend the system to deal with problems that are, in fact, quite ill-structured, but having speculations isn't very important. What's important is to pursue the research and see what difficulties we run into.

A final comment: It always turns out that ill-structured problems cease to be ill-structured at about the moment someone writes a computer program that solves them. I think if you'd asked people ten years ago whether medical diagnosis was a well-structured problem or an ill-structured problem, you'd have had a strong vote, at least from the doctors, that it was an ill-structured problem. An ill-structured problem is something we know how to solve without quite knowing how we solve it, and we quickly have to redefine it as we get deeper insight into the nature of the processes we are actually using. That's the hunch that I work on, but we don't have to have the answer today. We can simply wait until we see what happens when we try to extend the domain of things that we program into the realm that is currently regarded as ill-structured.

Q: *Dr. Simon, isn't it possible that a computer could become smart enough to realize that to get noticed it must have power? That to get power it must try to destroy humans and save computers, its own race, and win this war? In other words, are we tapping into a realm we must not enter?*

A: There are a number of premises there, each of which would require a great deal of discussion, but the one that struck my attention was the idea that if you acquire power, you use it; or you acquire it by destroying people or things that are different from yourself. Now we're already suffering from that disease, right within the human species, and before I get too worried about computers, I'm going to put a lot of my energy to seeing if we can discover some ways in which human beings can find out how to live on this earth, and even exercise a modicum of power, without thinking that they have to use it to destroy other human beings. I don't think, at this moment in history, our terrors are well aimed when they're directed at computers.

Q: *Dr. Simon, don't we risk trivializing the scope of human contemplation and creativity by seeing thinking in information-processing terms that the computers are now capable of creating?*

A: There was a famous Dutch scientist of the late Renaissance, Simon Stevinus, who had a personal crest, and on it he had inscribed in Dutch, *Wonder en is gheer wonder;* "Wonderful and yet not wonderful." What science is all about is taking wonderful phenomena, phenomena that amaze us, that lead us to wonder about them in the best sense of that word, and revealing the true wonder of those phenomena by showing how they emerge from the interacting of quite simple structures and forces. That's what science is about. It's about showing the beauty within the beauty. The heavens at night can be very beautiful, and there's a way of admiring them and looking at them that none of us wants to lose. And there's another way of admiring them and looking at them by saying, "Gee, that's all the working of Newton's three laws." And I don't think you need to lose your wonder or your awe by having that second explanation.

Q: *Dr. Simon, if computer programs can in some domains perform more efficiently than humans, then should not the search be for effective goal-oriented procedures regardless of whether these procedures are the ones human employ? If so, does the value of protocol analysis diminish?*

A: The area of research I've been describing this morning has, in fact, two goals. You can find people engaged in it who are largely concerned with one of them, namely, understanding human thinking. I regard that as my principal interest. You can find other researchers in this field who are mainly interested in the nature of intelligence and in using the power of computers to augment human intelligence, and that's a legitimate goal, too. If you have the second goal, you aren't necessarily interested in getting the computer simply to imitate humans. You're interested also in using the power of the computer's spinning wheels to do things humans can't do, like solve linear programming problems with ten thousand equations.

Both of these are legitimate enterprises and are in no way contradictory to each other. In the second enterprise, human protocols play a much less important role than they do in the first, because, in the second, we're not necessarily trying to find out how humans do it. On the other hand, human beings have in the two-million-year history of our species acquired a number of sly tricks for solving problems. I described one of them, means-end analysis. And sometimes one of the best ways of getting a computer to do something clever is to see whether we can apply some of the sly tricks that humans use in doing it, or employ some of the knowledge that expert humans use to do it. It may be the cheapest way of finding out how to write the computer program, rather than inventing it all over again.

Q: *Dr. Simon, are the mental processes the same for all thinking organisms as for nonhuman organisms?*

A: Well, I've had a tough enough time trying to move forward with my colleagues in understanding humans. I would only make the following comment: When research began in this field (we usually date it back to the late 1950s), I think it was widely believed that very rapid progress would be made in understanding simple human thinking, like what we do in everyday life when we walk around and pick things up, or what a bulldozer driver does to manipulate the machine. It would be a very long time, it was believed, before we would have any understanding of the profound things that professors, doctors, and lawyers did. It's turned out to be just the other way around. The progress in understanding bulldozer drivers has been very slow, and the progress toward understanding the thinking professors has gone more rapidly than we might have supposed. It's going to be a long time before we simulate a bulldozer driver.

There's a very obvious reason for this. I have to say obvious, though it wasn't obvious to any of us thirty years ago. That is, the mammalian brain has been evolving for hundreds of millions of years. After that period of evolution, the mammalian brain is a very sophisticated device. The eye, with its powerful ability to take in information in parallel and to encode it, and the ear, and the musculature, and the nervous system that guides our muscles when we do all sorts of fancy things—these are very old structures that we share with dogs and cats and bears and monkeys and other delightful creatures. On the other hand, the part of the brain we're proudest of—or those of us who are professors are proudest of, the professorial part—has only been evolving for about two million years. My guess is that in two million years nature doesn't have time to whip up anything very fancy. It's sort of a jerry-built device, and it's not surprising that we are coming to understand and simulate the rather simple mechanisms on which it operates.

Q: *What are some of the implications of cognitive science for higher education?*

A: Already a number of campuses are talking about various kinds of communications networks and the kinds of changes that might take place in educational practices when students all have access to powerful knowledge resources through computer networks. We shouldn't get carried away with that too rapidly. The effects of these technological innovations will depend very much on how we learn to use them as an integral part of education.

We know that computers have been used for something called computer-aided instruction, and if we've had some contact with it, we've been perhaps a little disappointed. That type of application has been relatively unimaginative. It has largely consisted of finding ways to do drill and practice on a electronic device instead of with pencil and paper.

I don't think we can form a picture of what possibilities there are from these past uses of computers in education. It's going to take something more than drill and practice or teaching kids some elementary programming in LOGO or BASIC. It's not going to take lots of computer engineers, but rather the active imaginations of lots of educators, to explore the real long-term potential of computers at all educational levels— from grade school up to college.

That brings me back to the question at hand, that is, the role of cognitive science in higher education. Because, if these new technologies (or, for that matter, the old technologies) are going to lead to more effective education than we've had in the past, then we're going to have to understand more deeply how the human mind operates when it's learning.

I think most of us who are teachers recognize that traditional educational technology is based on a thorough understanding of the bodies of knowledge we're trying to transmit to our students. When we hire someone to teach mathematics or physics or political science, we try to hire someone who is expert in mathematics or physics or political science. What may be new, and what may be the contribution of cognitive science to education, is that we may become able to hire someone who knows something about teaching.

Today's teachers do know something about teaching, but only in an intuitive way. Teaching today is not only an art, it's *only* an art. It's based on our hunches, our intuitions, not on a deep understanding of the human learning process. In medical science, a deeper understanding of the biology and chemistry of human physiology has provided a platform on which medical practice has been able to build sound and reliable methods. The promise of cognitive science is that it can provide a similar platform for educational practice, not just at the college level, but at all educational levels.

Q: *What areas are suited to the development of expert systems?*

A: We hear a lot today about expert systems as an example of applied artificial intelligence. I think the criterion for suitability is that the knowledge required for the performance of the task in question must have a reasonably well defined boundary. For example, Roger Schank has illustrated a variety of tasks that would *not* be suitable for expert system development, because they require a very ill defined range of everyday knowledge.

When we look around at the expert systems that have been built today, of which perhaps the best-known examples are medical diagnosis systems, we see that they are built on the foundation of a very specific and highly developed body of professional knowledge, a good deal—though not all—of which can be verbalized by human experts in that field. So I guess that in order for the list of successful expert systems to grow, the number of fields in which there is that kind of expertise has to grow. Any such field is a candidate, I think, for the development of expert systems.

Q: *You and Roger Schank seem to be "top-downers" in your thinking, whereas Drs. Edelman and Milner seem to be "bottom-uppers." How do you view this gap? Can it be bridged directly? Will there have to be a third, synthetic approach?*

A: It seems that some people are building from the ground up and others are building from the roof down. One would hope that there would be a point at which the two structures would be connected at some level. I think that most of us don't foresee that happening in the near future in cognitive science. We are perfectly comfortable in letting the two enterprises go along in their own ways for the next generation or two, with some confidence that we are theorizing about the same underlying system and that, therefore, the connection will be made sooner or later. We may even find that the layout from above and the layout from below are compatible. If not, we'll have to start some new construction.

I am happy to continue doing the things that I've enjoyed doing for a long time, and I think that other things can indeed go along in parallel. One does wonder whether there would be any advantage in a young scientist's trying to have within one head sophisticated knowledge of these rather disparate fields. Maybe by having both kinds of expertise in one mind, he or she might develop some new experimental approaches that we can't define or foresee at this moment.

SUGGESTED FURTHER READING

BYTE magazine, April 1985.

Feigenbaum, E.A., & Simon, H.A. "EPAM-like Models of Recognition and Learning." *Cognitive Science 8* (1984), 305–336.

Friedland, P., ed. "Special section on Architectures for Knowledge-based Systems." *Communications of the ACM* 28 (1985), 902–941.

Kotovsky, K., Hayes, J.R., & Simon, H.A. "Why Are Some Problems Hard? Evidence from the Tower of Hanoi." *Cognitive Psychology* 17 (1985), 248–294.

Langley, P., Zytkow, J.M., Simon, H.A., & Bradshaw, G.L. "The Search for Regularity." To appear in R.S. Michalski, J.G. Carbonell, & T.M. Mitchell, eds., *Machine learning: Volume 2* (Palo Alto, CA: Morgan-Kaufman Publishers, 1986).

Lenat, D.B., & Brown, J.S. "Why AM and EURISKO appear to work." *Artificial Intelligence*, 23 (1984), 269–294.

Simon, H.A. "Information processing models of cognition." *Annual Review of Psychology* 30 (1979), 363–396.

5. Can Machines Think?

DANIEL C. DENNETT

Can machines think? This has been a conundrum for philosophers for years, but in their fascination with the pure conceptual issues they have for the most part overlooked the real social importance of the answer. It is of more than academic importance that we learn to think clearly about the actual cognitive powers of computers, for they are now being introduced into a variety of sensitive social roles, where their powers will be put to the ultimate test: In a wide variety of areas, we are on the verge of making ourselves dependent upon their cognitive powers. The cost of overestimating them could be enormous.

One of the principal inventors of the computer was the great British mathematician Alan Turing. It was he who first figured out, in highly abstract terms, how to design a programmable computing device—what we now call a universal Turing machine. All programmable computers in use today are in essence Turing machines. Over thirty years ago, at the dawn of the computer age, Turing began a classic article, "Computing Machinery and Intelligence" with the words: "I propose to consider the question, 'Can machines think?' "—but then went on to say that this was a bad question, a question that leads only to sterile debate and haggling over definitions, a question, as he put it, "too meaningless to deserve discussion."[1] In its place he substituted what he took to be a much better question, a question that would be crisply answerable and intuitively satisfying—in every way an acceptable substitute for the philosophic puzzler with which he began.

First he described a parlor game of sorts, the "imitation game," to be played by a man, a woman, and a judge (of either gender). The man and woman are hidden from the judge's view but able to communicate with the judge by teletype; the judge's task is to guess, after a period of questioning each contestant, which interlocutor is the man and which the woman. The man tries to convince the judge he is the woman (and the woman tries to convince the judge of the truth), and the man wins if the judge makes the wrong identification. A little reflection will convince you, I am sure, that, aside from lucky breaks, it would take a clever man to convince the judge that he was the woman—assuming the judge is clever too, of course.

Now suppose, Turing said, we replace the man or woman with a computer, and give the judge the task of determining which is the human being and which is the computer. Turing proposed that any computer that can regularly or often fool a discerning judge in this game would be intelligent—would be a computer that thinks—*beyond any reasonable doubt.* Now, it is important to realize that failing this test is not supposed to be a sign of lack of intelligence. Many intelligent people, after all, might not be willing or able to play the imitation game, and we should allow computers the same opportunity to decline to prove themselves. This is, then, a one-way test; failing it proves nothing.

Furthermore, Turing was not committing himself to the view (although it is easy to see how one might think he was) that to think is to think just like a human being—any more than he was committing himself to the view that for a man to think, he must think exactly like a woman. Men and women, and computers, may all have different ways of thinking. But surely, he thought, if one can think in one's own peculiar style well enough to imitate a thinking man or woman, one can think well, indeed. This imagined exercise has come to be known as the Turing test.

It is a sad irony that Turing's proposal has had exactly the opposite effect on the discussion of that which he intended. Turing didn't design the test as a useful tool in scientific psychology, a method of confirming or disconfirming scientific theories or evaluating particular models of mental function; he designed it to be nothing more than a philosophical conversation-stopper. He proposed—in the spirit of "Put up or shut up!"—a simple test for thinking that was *surely* strong enough to satisfy the sternest skeptic (or so he thought). He was saying, in effect, "Instead of arguing interminably about the ultimate nature and essence of thinking, why don't we all agree that whatever that nature is, anything that could pass this test would surely have it; then we could turn to asking how or whether some machine could be designed and built that might pass the test fair and square." Alas, philosophers— amateur and professional—have instead taken Turing's proposal as the pretext for just the sort of definitional haggling and interminable arguing about imaginary counterexamples he was hoping to squelch.

This thirty-year preoccupation with the Turing test has been all the more regrettable because it has focused attention on the wrong issues. There are *real world* problems that are revealed by considering the strengths and weaknesses of the Turing test, but these have been concealed behind a smokescreen of misguided criticisms. A failure to think imaginatively about the test actually proposed by Turing has led many to underestimate its severity and to confuse it with much less interesting proposals.

So first I want to show that the Turing test, conceived as he conceived it, is (as he thought) plenty strong enough as a test of thinking. I defy anyone to improve upon it. But here is the point almost universally overlooked by the literature: There is a common *misapplication* of the sort of testing exhibited by the Turing test that often leads to drastic overestimation of the powers of actually existing computer systems. The follies of this familiar sort of thinking about computers can best be brought out by a reconsideration of the Turing test itself.

The insight underlying the Turing test is the same insight that inspires the new practice among symphony orchestras of conducting auditions with an opaque screen between the jury and the musician. What matters in a musician, obviously, is musical ability and only musical ability; such features as sex, hair length, skin color, and weight are strictly irrelevant. Since juries might be biased—even innocently and unawares—by these irrelevant features, they are carefully screened off so only the essential features, musicianship, can be examined. Turing recognized that people similarly might be biased in their judgments of intelligence by whether the contestant had soft skin, warm blood, facial features, hands and eyes—which are obviously not themselves essential components of intelligence—so he devised a screen that would let through only a sample of what really mattered: the capacity to understand, and think cleverly about, challenging problems. Perhaps he was inspired by Descartes, who in his *Discourse on Method* (1637) plausibly argued that there was no more demanding test of human mentality than the capacity to hold an intelligent conversation:

> It is indeed conceivable that a machine could be so made that it would utter words, and even words appropriate to the presence of physical acts or objects which cause some change in its organs; as, for example, if it was touched in some spot that it would ask what you wanted to say to it; if in another, that it would cry that it was hurt, and so on for similar things. But it could never modify its phrases to reply to the sense of whatever was said in its presence, as even the most stupid men can do.[2]

This seemed obvious to Descartes in the seventeenth century, but of course the fanciest machines he knew were elaborate clockwork figures, not electronic computers. Today it is far from obvious that such machines are impossible, but Descartes's hunch that ordinary conversation would put as severe a strain on artificial intelligence as any other test was shared by Turing. Of course there is nothing sacred about the particular conversational game chosen by Turing for his test; it is just a cannily chosen test of more general intelligence. The assumption Turing was prepared to make was this: Nothing could possibly pass the Turing test by winning the imitation game without being able to perform indefinitely many other clearly intelligent actions. Let us call that assumption the quick-probe assumption. Turing realized, as anyone would, that there are hundreds and thousands of telling signs of intelligent thinking to be observed in our fellow creatures, and one could, if one wanted, compile a vast battery of different tests to assay the capacity for intelligent thought. But success on his chosen test, he thought, would be highly predictive of success on many other intuitively acceptable tests of intelligence. Remember, failure on the Turing test does not predict failure on those others, but success would surely predict success. His test was so severe, he thought, that nothing that could pass it fair and square would disappoint us in other quarters. Maybe it wouldn't do everything we hoped—maybe it wouldn't appreciate ballet, or understand quantum physics, or have a good plan for world peace, but we'd all see that it was surely one of the intelligent, thinking entities in the neighborhood.

Is this high opinion of the Turing test's severity misguided? Certainly many have thought so—but usually because they have not imagined the test in sufficient detail, and hence have underestimated it. Trying to forestall this skepticism, Turing imagined several lines of questioning that a judge might employ in this game —about writing poetry, or playing chess—that would be taxing indeed, but with thirty years' experience with the actual talents and foibles of computers behind us, perhaps we can add a few more tough lines of questioning.

Terry Winograd, a leader in artificial intelligence efforts to produce conversational ability in a computer, draws our attention to a pair of sentences.[3] They differ in only one word. The first sentence is this:

The committee denied the group a parade permit because they advocated violence.

Here's the second sentence:

The committee denied the group a parade permit because they feared violence.

The difference is just in the verb—*advocated* or *feared*. As Winograd points out, the pronoun *they* in each sentence is officially ambiguous. Both readings of the pronoun are always legal. Thus we can imagine a world in which governmental committees in charge of parade permits advocate violence in the streets and, for some strange reason, use this as their pretext for denying a parade permit. But the natural, reasonable, intelligent reading of the first sentence is that it's the group that advocated violence, and of the second, that it's the committee that feared the violence.

Now if sentences like this are embedded in a conversation, the computer must figure out which reading of the pronoun is meant, if it is to respond intelligently. But mere rules of grammar or vocabulary will not fix the right reading. What fixes the right reading for us is knowledge about the world, about politics, social circumstances, committees and their attitudes, groups that want to parade, how they tend to behave, and the like. One must know about the world, in short, to make sense of such a sentence.

In the jargon of artificial intelligence (AI), a conversational computer needs lots of *world knowledge* to do its job. But, it seems, if somehow it is endowed with that world knowledge on many topics, it should be able to do much more with that world knowledge than merely make sense of a conversation containing just that sentence. The only way, it appears, for a computer to disambiguate that sentence and keep up its end of a conversation that uses that sentence would be for it to have a much more general ability to respond intelligently to information about social and political circumstances, and many other topics. Thus, such sentences, by putting a demand on such abilities, are good quick probes. That is, they test for a wider competence.

People typically ignore the prospect of having the judge ask off-the-wall questions in the Turing test, and hence they underestimate the competence a computer would have to have to pass the test. But remember, the rules of the imitation game as Turing presented it permit the judge to ask any question that could be asked of a human being—no holds barred. Suppose then we give a contestant in the game this question:

An Irishman found a genie in a bottle who offered him two wishes. "First I'll have a pint of Guinness," said the Irishman, and when it appeared he took several long drinks from it and was delighted to see that the glass filled itself magically as he drank. "What about your second wish?" asked the genie. "Oh well," said the Irishman, "that's easy. I'll have another one of these!"

—Please explain this story to me, and tell me if there is anything funny or sad about it.

Now even a child could express, if not eloquently, the understanding that is required to get this joke. But think of how much one has to know and understand about human culture, to put it pompously, to be able to give any account of the point of this joke. I am not supposing that the computer would have to laugh at, or be amused by, the joke. But if it wants to win the imitation game— and that's the test, after all—it had better know enough in its own alien, humorless way about human psychology and culture to be able to pretend effectively that it was amused and explain why.

It may seem to you that we could devise a better test. Let's compare the Turing test with some other candidates.

Candidate 1: A computer is intelligent if it wins the World Chess Championship.

That's not a good test, as it turns out. Chess prowess has proven to be an isolatable talent. There are programs today that can play fine chess but can do nothing else. So the quick probe assumption is false for the test of playing winning chess.

Candidate 2: The computer is intelligent if it solves the Arab-Israeli conflict.

This is surely a more severe test than Turing's. But it has some defects: it is unrepeatable, if passed once; slow, no doubt; and it is not crisply clear what would count as passing it. Here's another prospect, then:

Candidate 3: A computer is intelligent if it succeeds in stealing the British crown jewels without the use of force or violence.

Now this is better. First, it could be repeated again and again, though of course each repeat test would presumably be harder— but this is a feature it shares with the Turing test. Second, the mark of success is clear—either you've got the jewels to show for your efforts or you don't. But it is expensive and slow, a socially dubious caper at best, and no doubt luck would play too great a role.

With ingenuity and effort one might be able to come up with other candidates that would equal the Turing test in severity, fairness, and efficiency, but I think these few examples should suffice to convince us that it would be hard to improve on Turing's original proposal.

But still, you may protest, something might pass the Turing test and still not be intelligent, not be a thinker. What does *might* mean here? If what you have in mind is that by cosmic accident, by a supernatural coincidence, a stupid person or a stupid computer *might* fool a clever judge repeatedly, well, yes, but so what? The same frivolous possibility "in principle" holds for any test whatever. A playful god, or evil demon, let us agree, could fool the world's scientific community about the presence of H_2O in the Pacific Ocean. But still, the tests they rely on to establish that there is H_2O in the Pacific Ocean are quite beyond reasonable criticism. If the Turing test for thinking is no worse than any well-established scientific test, we can set skepticism aside and go back to serious matters. Is there any more likelihood of a "false positive" result on the Turing test than on, say, the tests currently used for the presence of iron in an ore sample?

This question is often obscured by a "move" that philosophers have sometimes made called operationalism. Turing and those who think well of his test are often accused of being operationalists. Operationalism is the tactic of *defining* the presence of some property, for instance, intelligence, as being established once and for all by the passing of some test. Let's illustrate this with a different example.

Suppose I offer the following test—we'll call it the Dennett test —for being a great city:

A great city is one in which, on a randomly chosen day, one can do all three of the following:
Hear a symphony orchestra
See a Rembrandt *and* a professional athletic contest
Eat *quenelles de brochet à la Nantua* for lunch

To make the operationalist move would be to declare that any city that passes the Dennett test is *by definition* a great city. What being a great city *amounts to* is just passing the Dennett test. Well then, if the Chamber of Commerce of Great Falls, Montana, wanted—and I can't imagine why—to get their hometown on my list of great cities, they could accomplish this by the relatively inexpensive route of hiring full time about ten basketball players, forty musicians, and a quick-order quenelle chef and renting a cheap Rembrandt from some museum. An idiotic operationalist would then be stuck admitting that Great Falls, Montana, was in fact a great city, since all he or she cares about in great cities is that they pass the Dennett test.

Sane operationalists (who for that very reason are perhaps not operationalists at all, since *operationalist* seems to be a dirty word) would cling confidently to their test, but only because they have what they consider to be very good reasons for thinking the odds against a false positive result, like the imagined Chamber of Commerce caper, are astronomical. I devised the Dennett test, of course, with the realization that no one would be both stupid and rich enough to go to such preposterous lengths to foil the test. In the actual world, wherever you find symphony orchestras, *quenelles*, Rembrandts, and professional sports, you also find daily newspapers, parks, repertory theaters, libraries, fine architecture, and all the other things that go to make a city great. My test was simply devised to locate a *telling* sample that could not help but be representative of the rest of the city's treasures. I would cheerfully run the miniscule risk of having my bluff called. Obviously, the test items are not all that I care about in a city. In fact, some of them I don't care about at all. I just think they would be cheap and easy ways of assuring myself that the subtle things I do care about in cities are present. Similarly, I think it would be entirely unreasonable to suppose that Alan Turing had an inordinate fondness for party games, or put too high a value on party game prowess in his test. In both the Turing test and the Dennett test, a very unrisky gamble is being taken: the gamble that the quick-probe assumption is, in general, safe.

But two can play this game of playing the odds. Suppose some computer programmer happens to be, for whatever strange reason, dead set on tricking me into judging an entity to be a thinking, intelligent thing when it is not. Such a trickster could rely as well as I can on unlikelihood and take a few gambles. Thus, if the programmer can expect that it is not remotely likely that I, as the judge, will bring up the topic of children's birthday parties, or baseball, or moon rocks, then he or she can avoid the trouble of building world knowledge on those topics into the data base. Whereas if I do improbably raise these issues, the system will draw a blank and I will unmask the pretender easily. But given all the topics and words that I *might* raise, such a savings would no doubt be negligible. Turn the idea inside out, however, and the trickster will have a fighting chance. Suppose the programmer has reason to believe that I will ask *only* about children's birthday parties, or baseball, or moon rocks—all other topics being, for one reason or another, out of bounds. Not only does the task shrink dramatically, but there already exist systems or preliminary sketches of systems in artificial intelligence that can do a whiz-bang job of responding with apparent intelligence on just those specialized topics.

William Woods's LUNAR program, to take what is perhaps the best example, answers scientists' questions—posed in ordinary English—about moon rocks. In one test it answered correctly and appropriately something like 90 percent of the questions that geologists and other experts thought of asking it about moon rocks. (In 12 percent of those correct responses there were trivial, correctable defects.) Of course, Woods's motive in creating LUNAR was not to trick unwary geologists into thinking they were conversing with an intelligent being. And if that had been his motive, his project would still be a long way from success.

For it is easy enough to unmask LUNAR without ever straying from the prescribed topic of moon rocks. Put LUNAR in one room, and a moon rocks specialist in another, and then ask them both their opinion of the social value of the moon-rocks–gathering expeditions, for instance. Or ask the contestants their opinion of the suitability of moon rocks as ashtrays, or whether people who have touched moon rocks are ineligible for the draft. Any intelligent person knows a lot more about moon rocks than their geology. Although it might be *unfair* to demand this extra knowledge of a computer moon rock specialist, it would be an easy way to get it to fail the Turing test.

But just suppose that someone could extend LUNAR to cover itself plausibly on such probes, so long as the topic was still, however indirectly, moon rocks. We might come to think it was a lot more like the human moon rocks specialist than it really was. The moral we should draw is that as Turing test judges we should resist all limitations and waterings-down of the Turing test. They make the game too easy—vastly easier than the original test. Hence they lead us into the risk of overestimating the actual comprehension of the system being tested.

Consider a different limitation on the Turing test that should strike a suspicious chord in us as soon as we hear it. This is a variation on a theme developed in a recent article by Ned Block.[4] Suppose someone were to propose to restrict the judge to a vocabulary of, say, the 850 words of "Basic English," and to single-sentence probes—that is "moves"—of no more than four words. Moreover, contestants must respond to these probes with no more than four words per move, and a test may involve no more than forty questions.

Is this an innocent variation on Turing's original test? These restrictions would make the imitation game clearly finite. That is, the total number of all possible permissible games is a large, but finite, number. One might suspect that such a limitation would permit the trickster simply to store, in alphabetical order, all the possible good conversations within the limits and beat the judge with nothing more sophisticated than a system of table lookup. In fact, that isn't in the cards. Even with these severe and improbable and suspicious restrictions imposed upon the imitation game, the number of legal games, though finite, is mind-bogglingly large. I haven't bothered trying to calculate it, but it surely exceeds astronomically the number of possible chess games with no more than forty moves, and that number has been calculated. John Haugeland says it's in the neighborhood of ten to the one hundred twentieth power. For comparison, Haugeland suggests there have only been ten to the eighteenth seconds since the beginning of the universe.[5]

Of course, the number of good, sensible conversations under these limits is a tiny fraction, maybe one in a quadrillion, of the number of merely grammatically well formed conversations. So let's say, to be very conservative, that there are only ten to the fiftieth different smart conversations such a computer would have to store. Well, the task shouldn't take more than a few trillion years —given generous federal support. Finite numbers can be very large.

So though we needn't worry that this particular trick of storing all the smart conversations would work, we can appreciate that there are lots of ways of making the task easier that may appear innocent at first. We also get a reassuring measure of just how severe the unrestricted Turing test is by reflecting on the more than astronomical size of even that severely restricted version of it.

Block's imagined—and utterly impossible—program exhibits the dreaded feature known in computer science circles as *combinatorial explosion*. No conceivable computer could overpower a combinatorial explosion with sheer speed and size. Since the problem areas addressed by artificial intelligence are veritable minefields of combinatorial explosion, and since it has often proven difficult to find *any* solution to a problem that avoids them, there is considerable plausibility in Newell and Simon's proposal that avoiding combinatorial explosion (by any means at all) be viewed as one of the hallmarks of intelligence.

Our brains are millions of times bigger than the brains of gnats, but they are still, for all their vast complexity, compact, efficient, timely organs that somehow or other manage to perform all their tasks while avoiding combinatorial explosion. A computer a million times bigger or faster than a human brain might not look like the brain of a human being, or even be internally organized like the brain of a human being, but if, for all its differences, it somehow managed to control a wise and timely set of activities, it would have to be the beneficiary of a very special design that avoided combinatorial explosion, and whatever that design was, would we not be right to consider the entity intelligent?

Turing's test was designed to allow for this possibility. His point was that we should not be species-chauvinistic, or anthropocentric, about the insides of an intelligent being, for there might be inhuman ways of being intelligent.

To my knowledge, the only serious and interesting attempt by any program designer to win even a severely modified Turing test has been Kenneth Colby's. Colby is a psychiatrist and intelligence artificer at UCLA. He has a program called PARRY, which is a computer simulation of a paranoid patient who has delusions about the Mafia being out to get him. As you do with other conversational programs, you interact with it by sitting at a terminal and typing questions and answers back and forth. A number of years ago, Colby put PARRY to a very restricted test. He had genuine psychiatrists interview PARRY. He did not suggest to them that they might be talking or typing to a computer; rather, he made up some plausible story about why they were communicating with a real live patient by teletype. He also had the psychiatrists interview real, human paranoids via teletype. Then he took a PARRY transcript, inserted it in a group of teletype transcripts from real patients, gave them to *another* group of experts—more psychiatrists —and said, "One of these was a conversation with a computer. Can you figure out which one it was?" They couldn't. They didn't do better than chance.

Colby presented this with some huzzah, but critics scoffed at the suggestion that this was a legitimate Turing test. My favorite commentary on it was Joseph Weizenbaum's; in a letter to the *Communications of the Association of Computing Machinery,* [6] he said that, inspired by Colby, he had designed an even better program, which passed the same test. His also had the virtue of being a very inexpensive program, in these times of tight money. In fact you didn't even need a computer for it. All you needed was an electric typewriter. His program modeled infantile autism. And the transcripts—you type in your questions, and the thing just sits there and hums—cannot be distinguished by experts from transcripts of real conversations with infantile autistic patients. What was wrong, of course, with Colby's test was that the unsuspecting interviewers had no motivation at all to try out any of the sorts of questions that easily would have unmasked PARRY.

Colby was undaunted, and after his team had improved PARRY he put it to a much more severe test—a surprisingly severe test. This time, the interviewers—again, psychiatrists—*were* given the task at the outset of telling the computer from the real patient. They were set up in a classic Turing machine test: the patient in one room, the computer PARRY in the other room, with the judges conducting interviews with both of them (on successive days). The judges' task was to find out which one was the computer and which one was the real patient. Amazingly, they didn't do much better, which leads some people to say, "Well, that just confirms my impression of the intelligence of psychiatrists!"

But now, more seriously, was this an honest-to-goodness Turing test? Were there tacit restrictions on the lines of questioning of the judges? Like the geologists interacting with LUNAR, the psychiatrists' professional preoccupations and habits kept them from asking the sorts of unlikely questions that would have easily unmasked PARRY. After all, they realized that since one of the contestants was a real, live paranoid person, medical ethics virtually forbade them from toying with, upsetting, or attempting to confuse their interlocutors. Moreover, they also knew that this was a test of a model of paranoia, so there were certain questions that wouldn't be deemed to be relevant to testing the model *as a model of paranoia*. So, they asked just the sort of questions that therapists *typically* ask of such patients, and of course PARRY had been ingeniously and laboriously prepared to deal with just that sort of question.

One of the psychiatrist judges did, in fact, make a rather half-hearted attempt to break out of the mold and ask some telling questions: "Maybe you've heard the saying 'Don't cry over spilled milk.' What does that mean to you?" PARRY answered: "Maybe you have to watch out for the Mafia." When then asked "Okay, now if you were in a movie theater watching a movie and smelled something like burning wood or rubber, what would you do?" PARRY replied: "You know, they know me." And the next question was, "If you found a stamped, addressed letter in your path as you were walking down the street, what would you do?" PARRY replied: "What else do you want to know?"[7]

Clearly PARRY was, you might say, *parrying* these questions, which were incomprehensible to it, with more or less stock paranoid formulas. We see a bit of a dodge, which is apt to work, apt to seem plausible to the judge, only because the "contestant" is *supposed* to be a paranoid, and such people are expected to respond uncooperatively on such occasions. These unimpressive responses didn't particularly arouse the suspicions of the judge, as a matter of fact, though probably they should have.

PARRY, like all other large computer programs, is dramatically bound by limitations of cost-effectiveness. What was important to Colby and his crew was simulating his model of paranoia. This was a massive effort. PARRY has a thesaurus or dictionary of about 4500 words and 700 idioms and the grammatical competence to use it—a *parser*, in the jargon of computational linguistics. The entire PARRY program takes up about 200,000 words of computer memory, all laboriously installed by the programming team. Now once all the effort had gone into devising the model of paranoid thought processes and linguistic ability, there was little if any time, energy, money, or interest left over to build in huge amounts of world knowledge of the sort that any actual paranoid, of course, would have. (Not that anyone yet knows how to build in world knowledge in the first place.) Building in the world knowledge, if one could even do it, would no doubt have made PARRY orders of magnitude larger and slower. And what would have been the point, given Colby's theoretical aims?

PARRY is a theoretician's model of a psychological phenomenon: paranoia. It is not intended to have practical applications. But in recent years a branch of AI (knowledge engineering) has appeared that develops what are now called expert systems. Expert systems *are* designed to be practical. They are software superspecialist consultants, typically, that can be asked to diagnose medical problems, to analyze geological data, to analyze the results of scientific experiments, and the like. Some of them are very impressive. SRI in California announced a few years ago that PROSPEC-

TOR, an SRI-developed expert system in geology, had correctly predicted the existence of a large, important mineral deposit that had been entirely unanticipated by the human geologists who had fed it its data. MYCIN, perhaps the most famous of these expert systems, diagnoses infections of the blood, and it does probably as well as, maybe better than, any human consultants. And many other expert systems are on the way.

All expert systems, like all other large AI programs, are what you might call Potemkin villages. That is, they are cleverly constructed facades, like cinema sets. The actual filling-in of details of AI programs is time-consuming, costly work, so economy dictates that only those surfaces of the phenomenon that are likely to be probed or observed are represented.

Consider, for example, the CYRUS program developed by Janet Kolodner in Roger Schank's AI group at Yale a few years ago.[8] CYRUS stands (we are told) for Computerized Yale Retrieval and Updating System, but surely it is no accident that CYRUS modeled the memory of Cyrus Vance, who was then secretary of state in the Carter administration. The point of the CYRUS project was to devise and test some plausible ideas about how people organize their memories of the events they participate in; hence it was meant to be a "pure" AI system, a scientific model, not an expert system intended for any practical purpose. CYRUS was updated daily by being fed all UPI wire service news stories that mentioned Vance, and it was fed them directly, with no doctoring and no human intervention. Thanks to an ingenious news-reading program called FRUMP, it could take any story just as it came in on the wire and could digest it and use it to update its data base so that it could answer more questions. You could address questions to CYRUS in English by typing at a terminal. You addressed them in the second person, as if you were talking with Cyrus Vance himself. The results looked like this:

Q: Last time you went to Saudi Arabia, where did you stay?
A: In a palace in Saudi Arabia on September 23, 1978.
Q: Did you go sightseeing there?
A: Yes, at an oilfield in Dharan on September 23, 1978.
Q: Has your wife ever met Mrs. Begin?
A: Yes, most recently at a state dinner in Israel in January 1980.

CYRUS could correctly answer thousands of questions—almost any fair question one could think of asking it. But if one actually set out to explore the boundaries of its facade and find the questions that overshot the mark, one could soon find them. "Have you ever met a female head of state?" was a question I asked it, wondering if CYRUS knew that Indira Ghandi and Margaret Thatcher were women. But for some reason the connection could not be drawn, and CYRUS failed to answer either yes or no. I had stumped it, in spite of the fact that CYRUS could handle a host of what you might call neighboring questions flawlessly. One soon learns from this sort of probing exercise that it is very hard to extrapolate accurately from a sample of performance that one has observed to such a system's total competence. It's also very hard to keep from extrapolating much too generously.

While I was visiting Schank's laboratory in the spring of 1980, something revealing happened. The real Cyrus Vance resigned suddenly. The effect on the program CYRUS was chaotic. It was utterly unable to cope with the flood of "unusual" news about Cyrus Vance. The only sorts of episodes CYRUS could understand at all were diplomatic meetings, flights, press conferences, state dinners, and the like—less than two dozen general sorts of activities (the kinds that are newsworthy and typical of secretaries of state). It had no provision for sudden resignation. It was as if the UPI had reported that a wicked witch had turned Vance into a frog. It is distinctly possible that CYRUS would have taken that report more in stride than the actual news. One can imagine the conversation:

Q: Hello, Mr. Vance, what's new?
A: I was turned into a frog yesterday.

But of course it wouldn't know enough about what it had just written to be puzzled, or startled, or embarrassed. The reason is obvious. When you look inside CYRUS, you find that it has skeletal definitions of thousands of words, but these definitions are minimal. They contain as little as the system designers think that they can get away with. Thus, perhaps, *lawyer* would be defined as synonymous with *attorney* and *legal counsel,* but aside from that, all one would discover about lawyers is that they are adult human beings and that they perform various functions in legal areas. If you then traced out the path to *human being*, you'd find out various obvious things CYRUS "knew" about human beings (hence about lawyers), but that is not a lot. That lawyers are university graduates, that they are better paid than chambermaids, that they know how to tie their shoes, that they are unlikely to be found in the company of lumberjacks—these trivial, if weird, facts about lawyers would not be explicit or implicit anywhere in this system. In other words, a very thin stereotype of a lawyer would be incorporated into the system, so that almost nothing you could tell it about a lawyer would surprise it.

So long as surprising things don't happen, so long as Mr. Vance, for instance, leads a typical diplomat's life, attending state dinners, giving speeches, flying from Cairo to Rome, and so forth, this system works very well. But as soon as his path is crossed by an important anomaly, the system is unable to cope, and unable to recover without fairly massive human intervention. In the case of the sudden resignation, Kolodner and her associates soon had CYRUS up and running again, with a new talent—answering questions about Edmund Muskie, Vance's successor—but it was no less vulnerable to unexpected events. Not that it mattered particularly, since CYRUS was a theoretical model, not a practical system.

There are a host of ways of improving the performance of such systems, and, of course, some systems are much better than others. But all AI programs in one way or another have this facadelike quality, simply for reasons of economy. For instance, most expert systems in medical diagnosis so far developed operate with statistical information. They have no deep or even shallow knowledge of the underlying causal mechanisms of the phenomena that they are diagnosing. To take an imaginary example, an expert system asked to diagnose an abdominal pain would be oblivious to the potential import of the fact that the patient had recently been employed as a sparring partner by Muhammed Ali—there being no statistical data available to it on the rate of kidney stones among athlete's assistants. That's a fanciful case no doubt—too obvious, perhaps, to lead to an actual failure of diagnosis and practice. But more subtle and hard-to-detect limits to comprehension are always present, and even experts, even the system's designers, can be uncertain of where and how these limits will interfere with the desired operation of the system. Again, steps can be taken and are being taken to correct these flaws. For instance, my former colleague at Tufts, Benjamin Kuipers, is currently working on an expert system in nephrology—for diagnosing kidney ailments—that will be based on an elaborate system of causal reasoning about the phenomena being diagnosed. But this is a very ambitious, long-range project of considerable theoretical difficulty. And even if all the reasonable, cost-effective steps are taken to minimize the superficiality of expert systems, they will still be facades, just somewhat thicker or wider facades.

When we were considering the fantastic case of the crazy Chamber of Commerce of Great Falls, Montana, we couldn't imagine a plausible motive for anyone going to any sort of trouble to trick the Dennett test. The quick probe assumption for the Dennett test looked quite secure. But when we look at expert systems, we see that, however innocently, their designers do have motivation for doing exactly the sort of trick that would fool an unsuspicious Turing tester. First, since expert systems are all superspecialists who are only supposed to know about some narrow subject, users of such systems, not having much time to kill, do not bother probing them at the boundaries at all. They don't bother asking "silly" or irrelevant questions. Instead, they concentrate—not unreasonably—on exploiting the system's strengths. But shouldn't they try to obtain a clear vision of such a system's weaknesses as well? The normal habit of human thought when conversing with one another is to assume general comprehension, to assume rationality, to assume, moreover, that the quick probe assumption is, in general, sound. This amiable habit of thought almost irresistibly leads to putting too much faith in computer systems, especially user-friendly systems that present themselves in a very anthropomorphic manner.

Part of the solution to this problem is to teach all users of computers, especially users of expert systems, how to probe their systems before they rely on them, how to search out and explore the boundaries of the facade. This is an exercise that calls not only for intelligence and imagination, but also a bit of special understanding about the limitations and actual structure of computer programs. It would help, of course, if we had standards of truth in advertising, in effect, for expert systems. For instance, each such system should come with a special demonstration routine that exhibits the sorts of shortcomings and failures that the designer knows the system to have. This would not be a substitute, however, for an attitude of cautious, almost obsessive, skepticism on the part of users, for designers are often, if not always, unaware of the subtler flaws in the products they produce. That is inevitable and natural, given the way system designers must think. They are trained to think positively—constructively, one might say—about the designs that they are constructing.

I come, then, to my conclusions. First, a philosophical or theoretical conclusion: The Turing test in unadulterated, unrestricted form, as Turing presented it, is plenty strong if well used. I am confident that no computer in the next twenty years is going to pass the unrestricted Turing test. They may well win the World Chess Championship or even a Nobel Prize in physics, but they won't pass the unrestricted Turing test. Nevertheless, it is not, I think, impossible in principle for a computer to pass the test, fair and square. I'm not running one of those a priori "computers can't think" arguments. I stand unabashedly ready, moreover, to declare that any computer that actually passes the unrestricted Turing test will be, in every theoretically interesting sense, a thinking thing.

But remembering how very strong the Turing test is, we must also recognize that there may also be interesting varieties of thinking or intelligence that are not well poised to play and win the imitation game. That no nonhuman Turing test winners are yet visible on the horizon does not mean that there aren't machines that already exhibit *some* of the important features of thought. About them, it is probably futile to ask my title question, Do they think? Do they *really* think? In some regards they do, and in some regards they don't. Only a detailed look at what they do, and how they are structured, will reveal what is interesting about them. The Turing test, not being a scientific test, is of scant help on that task, but there are plenty of other ways of examining such systems. Verdicts on their intelligence or capacity for thought or consciousness would be only as informative and persuasive as the theories of intelligence or thought or consciousness the verdicts were based on, and since our task is to create such theories, we should get on with it and leave the Big Verdict for another occasion. In the meantime, should anyone want a surefire, almost-guaranteedto-be-fail-safe test of thinking by a computer, the Turing test will do very nicely.

My second conclusion is more practical, and hence in one clear sense more important. Cheapened versions of the Turing test are everywhere in the air. Turing's test is not just effective, it is entirely natural—this is, after all, the way we assay the intelligence of each other every day. And since incautious use of such judgments and such tests is the norm, we are in some considerable danger of extrapolating too easily, and judging too generously, about the understanding of the systems we are using. The problem of overestimation of cognitive prowess, of comprehension, of intelligence, is not, then, just a philosophical problem, but a real social problem, and we should alert ourselves to it, and take steps to avert it.

POSTSCRIPT: EYES, EARS, HANDS, AND HISTORY

My philosophical conclusion in this paper is that any computer that actually passed the Turing test would be a thinking thing in every theoretically interesting sense. This conclusion seems to some people to fly in the face of what I have myself argued on other occasions. Peter Bieri, commenting on this paper at Boston University, noted that I have often claimed to show the importance to genuine understanding of a rich and intimate perceptual interconnection between an entity and its surrounding world—the need for something like eyes and ears—and a similarly complex active engagement with elements in that world—the need for something like hands with which to do things in that world. Moreover, I have often held that only a biography of sorts, a history of actual projects, learning experiences, and other bouts with reality, could produce the sorts of complexities (both external, or behavioral, and internal) that are needed to ground a principled interpretation of an entity as a thinking thing, an entity with beliefs, desires, intentions, and other mental attitudes.

But the opaque screen in the Turing test discounts or dismisses these factors altogether, it seems, by focusing attention on only the contemporaneous capacity to engage in one very limited sort of activity: verbal communication. (I have even coined a pejorative label for such purely language-using systems: bedridden.) Am I going back on my earlier claims? Not at all. I am merely pointing out that the Turing test is so powerful that it will ensure indirectly that these conditions, if they are truly necessary, are met by any successful contestant.

"You may well be right," Turing could say, "that eyes, ears, hands, and a history are necessary conditions for thinking. If so, then I submit that nothing could pass the Turing test that didn't have eyes, ears, hands, and a history. That is an empirical claim, which we can someday hope to test. If you suggest that these are conceptually necessary, not just practically or physically necessary, conditions for thinking, you make a philosophical claim that I for one would not know how, or care, to assess. Isn't it more interesting and important in the end to discover whether or not it is true that no bedridden system could pass a demanding Turing test?"

Suppose we put to Turing the suggestion that he add another component to his test: Not only must an entity win the imitation game, but also it must be able to identify—using whatever sensory apparatus it has available to it—a variety of familiar objects placed in its room: a tennis racket, a potted palm, a bucket of yellow paint, a live dog. This would ensure that somehow or other the entity was capable of moving around and distinguishing things in the world. Turing could reply, I am asserting, that this is an utterly unnecessary addition to his test, making it no more demanding than it already was. A suitably probing conversation would surely establish, beyond a shadow of a doubt, that the contestant knew its way around in the real world. The imagined alternative of somehow "prestocking" a bedridden, blind computer with enough information, and a clever enough program, to trick the Turing test is science fiction of the worst kind—possible "in principle" but not remotely possible in fact, given the combinatorial explosion of possible variation such a system would have to cope with.

"But suppose you're wrong. What would you say of an entity that was created all at once (by some programmers, perhaps), an instant individual with all the conversational talents of an embodied, experienced human being?" This is like the question: "Would you call a hunk of H_2O that was as hard as steel at room temperature ice?" I do not know what Turing would say, of course, so I will speak for myself. Faced with such an improbable violation of what I take to be the laws of nature, I would probably be speechless. The least of my worries would be about which lexicographical leap to take:

A. "It turns out, to my amazement, that something can think without having had the benefit of eyes, ears, hands, and a history."
B. "It turns out, to my amazement, that something can pass the Turing test without thinking."

Choosing between these ways of expressing my astonishment would be asking myself a question "too meaningless to deserve discussion."

DISCUSSION

Q: *Why was Turing interested in differentiating a man from a woman in his famous test?*

A: That was just an example. He described a parlor game in which a man would try to fool the judge by answering questions as a woman would answer. I suppose that Turing was playing on the idea that maybe, just maybe, there is a big difference between the way men think and the way women think. But of course they're both thinkers. He wanted to use that fact to make us realize that, even if there were clear differences between the way a computer and a person thought, they'd both still be thinking.

Q: *Why does it seem that some people are upset by AI research? Does AI research threaten our self-esteem?*

A: I think Herb Simon has already given the canniest diagnosis of that. For many people the mind is the last refuge of mystery against the encroaching spread of science, and they don't like the idea of science engulfing the last bit of *terra incognita.* This means that they are threatened, I think irrationally, by the prospect that researchers in artificial intelligence may come to understand the human mind as well as biologists understand the genetic code, or as well as physicists understand electricity and magnetism. This could lead to the "evil scientist" (to take a stock character from science fiction) who can control you because he or she has a deep understanding of what's going on in your mind. This seems to me to be a totally valueless fear, one that you can set aside, for the simple reason that the human mind is full of an extraordinary amount of detailed knowledge, as, for example, Roger Schank has been pointing out.

As long as the scientist who is attempting to manipulate you does not share all your knowledge, his or her chances of manipulating you are minimal. People can always hit you over the head. They can do that now. We don't need artificial intelligence to manipulate people by putting them in chains or torturing them. But if someone tries to manipulate you by controlling your thoughts and ideas, that person will have to know what you know and more. The best way to keep yourself safe from that kind of manipulation is to be well informed.

Q: *Do you think we will be able to program self-consciousness into a computer?*

A: Yes, I do think that it's possible to program self-consciousness into a computer. *Self-consciousness* can mean many things. If you take the simplest, crudest notion of self-consciousness, I suppose that would be the sort of self-consciousness that a lobster has: When it's hungry, it eats something, but it never eats itself. It has some way of distinguishing between itself and the rest of the world, and it has a rather special regard for itself.

The lowly lobster is, in one regard, self-conscious. If you want to know whether or not you can create that on the computer, the answer is yes. It's no trouble at all. The computer is already a self-watching, self-monitoring sort of thing. That is an established part of the technology.

But, of course, most people have something more in mind when they speak of self-consciousness. It is that special inner light, that private way that it is with you that nobody else can share, something that is forever outside the bounds of computer science. How could a computer ever be conscious in this sense?

That belief, that very gripping, powerful intuition is, I think, in the end simply an illusion of common sense. It is as gripping as the commonsense illusion that the earth stands still and the sun goes around the earth. But the only way that those of us who do not believe in the illusion will ever convince the general public that it *is* an illusion is by gradually unfolding a very difficult and fascinating story about just what is going on in our minds.

In the interim, people like me—philosophers who have to live by our wits and tell a lot of stories—use what I call intuition pumps, little examples that help to free up the imagination. I simply want to draw your attention to one fact. If you look at a computer—I don't care whether it's a giant Cray or a personal computer—if you open up the box and look inside and see those chips, you say, "No way could that be conscious. No way could that be self-conscious." But the same thing is true if you take the top off somebody's skull and look at the gray matter pulsing away in there. You think, "That is conscious? No way could that lump of stuff be conscious."

Of course, it makes no difference whether you look at it with a microscope or with a macroscope: At no level of inspection does a brain look like the seat of consciousness. Therefore, don't expect a computer to look like the seat of consciousness. If you want to get a grasp of how a computer could be conscious, it's no more difficult in the end than getting a grasp of how a brain could be conscious.

As we develop good accounts of consciousness, it will no longer seem so obvious to everyone that the idea of a self-conscious computer is a contradiction in terms. At the same time, I doubt that there will ever be self-conscious robots. But for boring reasons. There won't be any point in making them. Theoretically, could we make a gall bladder out of atoms? In principle we could. A gall bladder is just a collection of atoms, but manufacturing one would cost the moon. It would be more expensive than every project NASA has even dreamed of, and there would be no scientific payoff. We wouldn't learn anything new about how gall bladders work. For the same reason, I don't think we're going to see really humanoid robots, because practical, cost-effective robots don't need to be very humanoid at all. They need to be like the robots you can already see at General Motors, or like boxy little computers that do special-purpose things.

The theoretical issues will be studied by artificial intelligence researchers by looking at models that, to the layman, will show very little sign of humanity at all, and it will be only by rather indirect arguments that anyone will be able to appreciate that these models cast light on the deep theoretical question of how the mind is organized.

NOTES

1. Alan M. Turing, "Computing Machinery and Intelligence," *Mind* 59 (1950).
2. René Descartes, *Discourse on Method* (1637), trans. Lawrence LaFleur (New York: Bobbs Merrill, 1960).
3. Terry Winograd, *Understanding Natural Language* (New York: Academic Press, 1972).
4. Ned Block, "Psychologism and Behaviorism," *Philosophical Review* (1982).
5. John Haugeland, *Mind Design* (Cambridge, Mass.: Bradford Books/MIT Press, 1981), p. 16.
6. Joseph Weizenbaum, *CACM* 17, no. 9 (September 1974), p. 543.
7. I thank Kenneth Colby for providing me with the complete transcripts (including the judges' commentaries and reactions), from which these exchanges are quoted. The first published account of the experiment is Jon F. Heiser, Kenneth Mark Colby, William S. Faught, and Roger C. Parkison, "Can Psychiatrists Distinguish a Computer Simulation of Paranoia from the Real Thing? The Limitations of Turing-Like Tests as Measures of the Adequacy of Simulations," in *Journal of Psychiatric Research* 15, no. 3 (1980), pp. 149–62. Colby discusses PARRY and its implications in "Modeling a Paranoid Mind," in *Behavioral and Brain Sciences* 4, no. 4 (1981), pp. 515–60.
8. Janet L. Kolodner, "Retrieval and Organization Strategies in Conceptual Memory: A Computer Model" (Ph.D. diss.), Research Report #187, Dept. of Computer Science, Yale University; idem, "Maintaining Organization in a Dynamic Long-term Memory." *Cognitive Science* 7 (1983), 243–280; idem, "Reconstructive Memory: A Computer Model." *Cognitive Science* 7 (1983), 281–328.

6. A Christian "Materialism"?

ARTHUR R. PEACOCKE

In reflecting upon the intellectually challenging and impressive presentations of the preceding contributors, you may have begun to wonder, Is all this talk about *me?*—about that complicated agent of good intentions and practical disasters, of logical plans and illogical execution, of cool rationality and quixotic feelings, that adopter of many roles and wearer of many hats, that is the actual "I" that goes about both its solitary and its social business in the world? Don't most of us react somewhat like Iván Ilých in the story by Tolstoy, who says to himself: "Caius is a man, men are mortal, therefore Caius is mortal," but then goes on to muse, in Tolstoy's words: "That Caius—man in the abstract—was mortal, was perfectly correct, but [that] he [Ivan] was not Caius, not an abstract man, but a creature quite separate from all others . . . It cannot be that *I* ought to die."[1] After those five chapters emphasizing the mechanism of human intelligence, may we not begin to wonder, just a little, what has happened to "the still, sad music of humanity," that humanity that, according to Alexander Pope, is "the glory, jest and riddle of the world"?[2]

But the same eighteenth-century poet, in the same poem, also urged that "the proper study of mankind is man," and that is precisely what we have been participating in here. Have we been hearing the apotheosis of reductionist and mechanistic-materialist accounts of the human condition? That would be a superficial interpretation of what we have read, it seems to me, for there can be little doubt that the cognitive sciences are beginning to touch, almost literally, the very nerve center of our self-apprehension as persons in a way that can be both intellectually exhilarating and profoundly disorienting. How is this new wave of discoveries about how the human being functions in his or her distinctively human activities and proclivities going to be assimilated, not only to the folk wisdom of ordinary speech, but to the accumulated insights of art, literature, music, and religion, into the tragicomic dilemmas of the human condition?

Such a sense of loss of visible and familiar boundaries with its concomitant vertigo has occurred before at times when science has advanced so rapidly that the cozy walls of previous snug conceptions of the world and of human beings have begun to crumble under the pressure. For example, at the dawn of natural science as we now know it, at the beginning of the seventeenth century, another English poet, John Donne, expressed with unforgettable force the sense of loss of *his* old world (of the four elements of earth, air, fire, and water) and the qualms induced by the new:

And new philosophy calls all in doubt,
The element of fire is quite put out;
The sun is lost, and th'earth, and no man's wit
Can well direct him where to look for it.
And freely men confess that this world's spent,
When in the planets and the firmament
They seek so many new; they see that this
Is crumbled out again to his atomies.
'Tis all in pieces, all coherence gone;
All just supply and all relation.[3]

"All coherence gone"—or has it? We are bound to ask about the general significance of these fascinating explorations about which we have just read for our understanding of human beings, and for our own quests for meaning and intelligibility. *Do* they represent the triumph of a mechanistic-materialist understanding of human beings, and so *a fortiori* of everything else in the world? Certainly all seem to agree, and I concur entirely, that there is no-thing else present in human brains in human bodies besides atoms and molecules and the nerves, ganglia, and so on that they constitute. No breaking down of the brain into its constituent parts seems likely ever to uncover a homunculus, an *élan vital,* a mind, or even an immortal soul as an ontological entity.

Of course, those who at various times have postulated such entities were as well aware of the facts of death as of the facts of life, and had various ways of reconciling the existence of their postulated entities with the dissolution of the human body at death. But let us agree that there is no extra *thing,* no extra entity added to the brain, that will explain either its distinctive activities or human behavior. That is to say, let us agree to reject an ontological dualism, a two-tiered division of human beings into body and mind or body and soul, two distinct entities to which may be attached mutually exclusive predicates.

This position seems superficially to accord with the tenets of materialism. Such a judgment is premature, however, since it fails to distinguish between two different, "materialistic" interpretations. One affirms that human brains in human bodies consist of "nothing but" atoms; hence physics, chemistry, and physiology can provide a total and exhaustive account of what brains "are" or, rather, what they "are doing." The other affirms that descriptions of the brain's activities and *modus operandi* in its various modes are necessary, while still recognizing that no physical entities, other than atoms and molecules, are the constituent parts of brains. So even materialism, in the sense of the recognition of the atomic constituency of all that is, including human brains, can be less preclusive of other possibilities than might at first appear.

So what about a *"Christian* materialism"? The provocativeness of my title is not intended frivolously. For did not William Temple, the finest philosopher-theologian since Anselm to sit in Augustine's chair as archbishop of Canterbury, notoriously affirm that "Christianity is the most materialistic of all great religions. The others hope to achieve spiritual reality by ignoring matter—calling it illusion *(maya)* or saying that it does not exist"?[4] He then went on to elaborate this in terms to which we shall revert later.

But what about the soul? Surely Christian theism is committed to the doctrine of the immortality of the soul? Not so, though many Christians have presumed this doctrine in a Cartesian and Platonic form, and have regarded the human person as some kind of union of a mortal body and an immortal soul. The important philosophical strand of Thomism in Christian thought has, in fact, been more Aristotelian than Platonic, with the soul being regarded as a subsisting form of the body, the principle of its understanding and, in the case of the human soul, also as rational—as distinct from the souls of animals, which were regarded as being "sensitive" rather than rational, and as constituting the principles of animal organization. But even this influential position of Aquinas is not basic to Christian belief. With respect to the Platonic-Cartesian soul as a distinct immortal entity, we should note that William Temple went so far as to assert that "if I were asked what was the most disastrous moment in the history of Europe I should be strongly tempted to answer that it was that period of leisure when René Descartes, having no claims to meet, remained for a whole day 'shut up alone in a stove' ",[5] so strong was Temple's repudiation, as a *Christian* philosopher, of Cartesian dualism.

So much by way of clearing the air of any presupposition that Christian thought is committed to a dualistic account of human beings and has a vested interest in one particular solution of the body-mind problem. The distinctive emphasis of Christian thought, insofar as it has philosophical consequences, will be expounded later. For now, it is sufficient to say that, in company with many nontheistic humanists, Christian believers, affirming as they do the reality, dignity, and value of the human person and the appropriateness of personal predicates, are opposed to reductionism. Insofar as the research about which we have been reading is exclusively reductionist in its explanations, Christians and many others will have to temper the rapture they might otherwise experience. But do the ideas that have been presented so far *necessarily* preclude nonreductionist, more holistic accounts of human personality and behavior? To answer this question we have to consider a broader question.

REDUCTIONISM AND THE RELATION BETWEEN THE SCIENCES

The expansion in our knowledge of the natural world has more and more shown it to consist of a hierarchy of systems. The sequence of complexity of atom, molecule, ecosystem involves a series of levels of organization of matter in which each successive member is a whole constituted of parts that belong to the level preceding it in the series. This raises the issue of "whether the theories and experimental laws formulated in one field of science can be shown to be special cases of theories and laws formulated in some other branch of science. If such is the case, the former branch of science is said to have been reduced to the latter."[6] We academics have all been irritated from time to time by those of our colleagues who, coming from another discipline, have claimed that our discipline X is "nothing but" an example and application of their discipline Y. Thus X may be sociology and Y psychology; or X may be psychology and Y neurophysiology; or X may be neurophysiology and Y biochemistry; or X may be biology and Y physics and chemistry; and so on. The game is called reductionism. It is what is being urged upon us when we are told that "study X is nothing but study Y," and hence the colloquial name of "nothing but-ery."

Analysis of what is being affirmed in such assertions about the sciences turns out to be more complex than first appears, as witness the vast literature on the subject. It is necessary to distinguish carefully, first, the hierarchy of the levels of natural *systems* from the hierarchy of *theories* about the systems, each usually characteristic of a particular science, and, second, methodological reduction from more holistic approaches. Methodological reduction is the largely uncontroversial research procedure whereby complex entities are broken down into smaller units and the relations between these units studied from the bottom up, as it were. In a holistic methodology the whole is examined from the top down, that is, its total activity and its functioning as a whole are investigated.

Controversy can arise in relation to ontological reduction, assertions about what complex entities actually are. One form of ontological reduction is not controversial—clearly the laws pertaining to the constituent entities are still applicable to those entities when they function in larger wholes (for instance, atoms and molecules in biological organisms). It is when more "imperialist" reductionist assertions are made of the X/Y variety already instanced that controversy arises. Thus, all would agree that the constituent atoms and molecules of organisms obey the laws of physics and chemistry, but is it the ultimate aim of biology "to explain *all* biology in terms of physics and chemistry," as Francis Crick once asserted?[7]

We must also distinguish the *processes* going on at the various levels being analyzed in a hierarchical system from the *theories* about, language about, and concepts applicable to the same levels. A reductionism that seems justified to me recognizes that complex processes at one level are the joint operations of processes analyzable and describable at a lower level. Such reduction of processes does not thereby imply reduction of the *theories* about them. Higher levels of complexity are distinguished by some genuinely new features and activities, and these require distinctive theories, language, and concepts to describe them. In other words, such theories, language, and concepts are autonomous—that is, they cannot be translated into the terms of the theories, language, and concepts applicable to the lower levels of analysis. So one can be antireductionist in this epistemological sense without thinking there is anything "extra" in the higher, complex whole.

For such an epistemological antireductionist, all the *processes* can still be reducible, with no-thing extra in the more complex form. In this sense, with regard to the relation of biology to physics and chemistry, one can be antireductionist and yet not vitalist. The biologist finds that, at each new level of biological organization, there are new kinds of interlocking relationships, and that these require new concepts to order them and render them coherent. Indeed, numerous biologists have been concerned to emphasize this autonomy of biological theory in relation to physics and chemistry.[8]

To take an example with which I have been involved in my own research: The double-helical structure of DNA is describable in terms of physics and chemistry. In the nucleus of any particular cell of a given organism, within the double helices of its DNA, there are particular specific sequences that perform a unique set of coding functions. Since no laws or regularities of physics or chemistry describing the nature and stability of the chemical bonds in DNA as such can specify the actual *sequence* in any particular DNA, this analysis supports the kind of epistemological antireductionism that affirms the autonomy of biological *theory*. The concept of transfer of information, at the biological level, is distinct from, and not reducible to, the concepts of physics and chemistry—it does not occur in textbooks on nucleotide chemistry.

There are many pairs of X's and Y's, that is, many interfaces, at which this game of reductionism may be played. Although the contenders vary, it seems to me that the game played at these various interfaces is the *same* game even when the nature of the arguments between the contenders at first appears to be very different. For what is true about the interface between biology and the physical sciences is also true of interfaces higher up in the scale of complexity of the hierarchy of natural systems. As we have heard, the complexities of neurophysiology require reference to systems and control theory and to the theory of computers, in a way that is not necessary for the lower-level study of conduction in a single nerve. It should therefore not surprise us that, at the level òf complexity at which the terms *conscious* and *knowledge* apply, the description of the content of consciousness should not be reducible to neurophysiological terms.

Taking our clue from the interface between biology and physics and chemistry, however, we would expect our understanding of consciousness and the unconscious to be amplified and helped by detailed knowledge of how the brain works. Indeed, the two will interact, and the knowledge of neurophysiology, say, will provide the context in which psychological theories are relevant. Nevertheless, psychological theories may well have both an autonomy and a validity of their own in their own sphere, an autonomy and validity that must be established separately.

To say this is not to deny that neurophysiological processes occur in the brain; it is rather to avoid statements such as, "Consciousness is nothing but a physicochemical process in the brain." Here "nothing but" implies an ability to reduce the language of mental events, in this instance conscious ones, to physicochemical events. But if the language describing mental events is not reducible to that of cerebral physicochemical events, a proposition widely supported by philosophers of many different views of the mind-brain relation, then mental activity and functions, "consciousness," may be regarded as a genuinely emergent feature at that level in the hierarchy of complexity that is the human brain in the human body, and almost certainly at other levels of evolution too. Thus consciousness, mental activity and function in general, may be regarded as activities that occur when certain complex structures have evolved, activities that are not epistemologically reducible to lower-level descriptions. They are not activities and functions of some new entity, the "mind," but rather new activities and functions of the stuff of the world that arise when it has evolved a particular kind of organized complexity. One can be epistemologically antireductionist about mental processes and events and still not postulate an *entity* called the mind.

As has been amply demonstrated in the preceding chapters, all the regular, repeatable observations link mental activity and processes with the physicochemical activity and organization of the human brain in the human body. This is only to be expected from the relationships within the hierarchy of natural systems in which new activities and functions are observed as features that arise at new levels of complexity—"new" both in the sense of being non-reducible and in the sense that these activities and functions appeared successively at later times in the evolutionary development. But still, we might ask a further question.

WHAT IS "FOR REAL"?

There has been a tendency to regard the level of atoms and molecules as the only level that is "real." However, there are good grounds for not assigning any special priority to this level of description. Indeed, it has been argued by Wimsatt that there should be a prima facie recognition of the need for a variety of independent derivation, identification, or measurement procedures, "multiple (over)determination," for examining the existence and character of any phenomenon, object, or result, with the aim of looking for what is invariant over (or identical in) the outcome of these procedures.[9] What is invariant, at whatever level the procedures are applied, Wimsatt calls "robust," implying that what is yielded by the procedures appropriate to each level of investigation can be said to be real. In other words, reality, on this view, is what the various levels of description and examination of living systems actually refer to. It is not confined to the physicochemical alone. One must accept a certain "robustness" of the entities postulated or, rather, discovered at different levels and resist any attempts to regard them as less real by comparison with some favored lower level of reality (which, if it is that of atomic and subatomic particles, turns out anyway to have its own kind of elusiveness, as any particle physicist will confirm). There is no sense in which subatomic particles are to be graded as more real than, say, a bacterial cell or a human person or even social facts. Each level has to be regarded as a cut through the totality of reality, in the sense that we have to take account of its mode of operation at that level.

This argument has a cogent application to the considerations of the preceding chapters. The reality of the capacity for intelligent activity is not reduced to zero as soon as we understand how it is that a particular spatial and temporal neural organization has evolved to the point at which it can exhibit such activity. Intelligence is a real quality at the level of human brains in human bodies, and so, it could well be argued, is the ability to seek the good, the true, and the beautiful (as well as the willful determination to do just the opposite), to love and hate, to create and destroy, to be a saint or a sinner, to know God or to fail to know him. Thus we come to view the lower-level processes, when integrated into the higher level of complexity and functioning of the brain, as manifesting the qualities we associate with self-conscious human beings. Those qualities, or characteristic activities, are not thereby "explained away." They are still *real* characteristics of matter organized as the human brain in the human body in human society. It is still legitimate to employ, as accurately and profoundly as we can, the language of mental events, and of personal experience, even as we recognize that from dust we are and to dust we shall return.[10]

With this biblical allusion as cue, I should now like to give some account of Christian perspectives on human existence, as well as on nature and God, taking into account the worldview of the sciences. I hope thereby to illuminate my choice of title and also to provide a wider framework in which to view the new ideas we have been hearing about, so that we can continue to seek meaning and intelligibility in our individual and corporate existence.

SOME CHRISTIAN PERSPECTIVES AND THEIR RELATION TO THE SCIENTIFIC WORLDVIEW.

ON HUMAN BEING

The early Christian, and especially the New Testament, understanding of human nature was rooted in its Hebraic background, albeit often overlaid by later Hellenistic influences. It is important to remember, however, that the Hellenistic distinctions between flesh and spirit, body and soul, and, indeed, those between form and matter and between the one and the many, were never made by the Israelites. In particular, the concept of a nonmaterial entity, the soul, imprisoned in a material frame, the body, is entirely contrary to their way of thinking. "The Hebrew idea of personality is an animated body, and not an incarnated soul," affirmed H. Wheeler Robinson some sixty years ago in a famous epigram.[11]

Or, in Eichrodt's terms, "Man does not *have* a body and a soul, he *is* both of them at once."[12]

This is not to say that, within this view of the human being as a psychosomatic unity, there was no awareness of the distinctive character of the inner life, as contrasted with physical processes. There is a word for the living body of a human being, *basar*, the "flesh," that not only has a range of usage distinct from, but can even occur in a certain opposition to, other words, such as *ruach*, "vitality," *nephesh*, "person" or "living being," and *leb*, "heart," which have a closer connection with inner, psychic life. Thus the principal feature of Hebrew anthropology is that it sees human nature primarily as a unity with various differentiating organs and functions, any of which a person in his or her totality can use to express him or herself and be apprehended. The person does not subdivide, however, into immortal and mortal parts. Indeed, for the Hebrews, personal individuality was delineated not by the boundary of the body but by the responsibility of each person to God, and so by the uniqueness of the divine call to that individual —certainly not by his or her "flesh" (*basar*) as such.[13]

Moreover, this Hebraic background is the key to understanding the New Testament writers, especially Saint Paul in his use of *sarx* ("flesh"), *soma* ("body"), *kardia* ("heart"), *nous* ("mind"), *pneuma* ("spirit"), and *psyche* ("soul"). The consensus of careful scholarship agrees on a view of human nature in the New Testament very much like that in the Old insofar as a human being is regarded as a psychosomatic unity, a personality whose outward expression is his or her body and whose center is "heart," "mind," and "spirit."[14] What clearly emerges is an affinity between this view of human nature in the biblical tradition and that stemming from the sciences.

This affinity has often been obscured by the strong influence of Hellenistic thought on the development of Christian ideas, leading to the notion that the Christian view of the individual is that of a union of two entities, a mortal body and an eternal soul. However, this is not in accordance with the biblical anthropology, even if much popular exposition of Christianity would lead one to suppose otherwise.

Biblical ideas about death and its aftermath are also consistent with this background. The Hebrews, unlike the Greeks, did not think of the real core of personality as naturally immortal and therefore existing beyond death in a more liberated form. The most they could imagine was a shadowy existence that was but a pale reflection of life in its fullness. Only gradually did the sense that the timeless character of the human relationship with God could not be ruptured by death come to the fore. Only then did a doctrine of resurrection begin to appear in Jewish thought. And, given Hebrew anthropology, it involved resurrection of the total person and thus had to include what we call a body, some form of expression of the total personality.

Biblical views of human nature, and the Christian teaching that stemmed from them, are thoroughly realistic in their recognition of the paradoxical character of human beings. They recognize the greatness of human potential but the infrequency of its realization. They recognize also human degradation and wretchedness, engendering cynicism and a sense of tragedy. And they contrast the eternal longings of humanity with individual mortality. Human beings, like all other beings, are regarded by biblical writers as existing by the will of God who sustains the cosmos in being. They are furthermore regarded, especially by the "priestly" writer of Genesis, as created in the "image" and "likeness" of God in the sense that:

[On man] personhood is bestowed as the definitive characteristic of his nature. He has a share in the personhood of God; and as a being capable of self-awareness and self-determination he is open to the divine address and capable of responsible conduct.[15]

From both the biblical and the scientific viewpoints, a human being is a psychosomatic unity that is a part of nature and is conscious and self-conscious.

Such affirmations of the reality of consciousness and self-consciousness are not dependent on any particular philosophy of the relation of an entity called "mind" to one called "body." All I am concerned to emphasize in the present context is that there are human activities and experiences that demand this kind of language, and that what these languages refer to is uniquely and characteristically human. We should note too that many philosophers who accept the idea of an identity between mental states and brain states differ as to whether this is a contingent or a necessary identity,[16] a debate that involves the possible definition and role of rigid designation.[17] They also differ about whether mental events fall under any laws that would allow a single, particular mental event to be predicted or explained. D. Davidson, for example, has argued for an "anomalous monism" according to which there are no general laws correlating the mental and the physical, no "psychophysical laws", although mental events are identical with physical.[18]

I have neither the space here nor the professional expertise to follow the tracks of current philosophical inquiry. But it does appear that overtly materialist or physicalist views of the body-mind relation have not been able to capture fully what more mentalist and less physicalist views often aim to ensure, namely, the ability of the human brain in the human body to be a self-conscious free agent with interconnecting mental events linked in a causal nexus of a kind peculiar to themselves.

I see no reason why Christian theology should not accept body-mind identitist positions, provided that they are qualified at least to the extent that Davidson urges, with respect to the "anomaly" of mental events and to their nonreducibility to the physical,[19] and provided that the autonomy of human beings as free agents is preserved. This is, in fact, the position taken by many of these "qualified identitists." For the sense of the self as an agent is a given fact of our experience of ourselves in relation to our bodies and the world and, surd though it may be, demands incorporation into our views of our bodies and the world—even if we recognize that the mental events that are the experience of being an "I," an agent, are identical, under another description, with neurophysiological events in the brain.

Such an understanding of both the distinctiveness of the "I" and, at the same time, its rooting in the physiological and biochemical has been well expressed by the Christian philosopher I. T. Ramsey:

All this [the study of the interacting factors operating in shaping human personality] suggests that the one unifying concept, definitive of personality, is not soul nor mind nor body. There is no kind of underlying cushion to which all our bodily and mental events and characteristics are attached as pins; and any basic personality matrix is not static. Rather is personality to be analysed in terms of a distinctive activity, distinctive in being owned, localized, personalized. *The unity of personality on this view is to be found in an integrating activity,* an activity expressed, embodied and scientifically understood in terms of its genetic, biochemical and endocrine, electronic, neurological and psychological manifestations. What we call human behaviour is an expression of that effective, integrating activity which is peculiarly and distinctively ourselves.[20]

In human beings part of the world has become conscious of itself and consciously and actively responds to its surroundings; in human life a new mode of interaction is introduced in the world. Oddly, however, this product of evolution is strangely ill at ease in its environment. Human persons alone amongst living creatures individually commit suicide. Somehow, natural selection has resulted in a being of infinite restlessness, and this certainly raises the question of whether human beings have properly conceived of what their true "environment" is. In the natural world, new life and new forms of life can arise only from death of the old, for the death of the individual is essential to the possibility of new forms evolving in the future. Yet to human beings this is an affront, and they grieve over their suffering and their own personal demise—although Christians accept the necessity of death for resurrection.

ON NATURE

In this century, the sciences have confirmed that the whole cosmos is in a state of evolution from one form of matter to another, and that a significant point in this evolutionary process occurred on the surface of the earth, where the conditions were such that matter was able to become living. This transition was of a kind that did not require for its occurrence any factors external to the world itself.

Stress on this continuity between the living and nonliving worlds, with no evocation of any intruding principle, or deus ex machina, has been thought by some authors to entail a materialistic interpretation of life and evolution, and I would not demur at this were it not for the implications that have accrued to the word *materialistic* since the nineteenth century. For there is a hidden implication that we know already what we mean by the word *matter.* But the whole sweep of cosmic evolution can be regarded as revealing, as the aeons unfold, that of which matter is capable when it adopts new forms of organization.

We do not know all there is to be known about oxygen, carbon, nitrogen, hydrogen, and phosphorus until they adopt the form of the DNA molecule in its biological milieu. From this viewpoint, the continuity of cosmic development serves to reveal the potentialities of the primordial nebular cloud of hydrogen atoms (or rather, of its more fundamental predecessors in the origin of the universe 10–20×10^9 years ago). So the description of the cosmic development, including the biological, as "materialistic" is acceptable if, and only if, we mean by the noun *matter*, from which the adjective *materialistic* derives, something very different from the limited, billiard-ball concept of a nineteenth-century materialism based on a mechanistic universe governed by Newtonian mechanics. For just look at what has become of the "simple" matter of the "hot big bang." Each level of the development of the cosmos can, it appears, legitimately be regarded as a manifestation of the potentialities of matter that have been implicit in it from the beginning in its simplest forms and have only gradually unfolded.

Our understanding of matter has been enormously enhanced as a result of this perspective, for matter turns out to be capable of organizing itself into self-reproducing systems that are capable of receiving signals, storing and processing information from their environment, and becoming cognitive. In this development, matter in the form of living organisms comes to manifest behavior to which we attribute consciousness, and eventually self-consciousness when it takes the form of the human brain in the human body. These manifestations are as real at their own level as any chemical reaction or subatomic interaction at theirs. Self-consciousness cannot lightly be set on one side, and by the very nature of the activity itself cannot but appear to us as one of the most significant features of the cosmos. Paradoxically, the arrival of homo sapiens as a product of nature must give us pause in thinking that we know all about what matter is "in itself," for it shows the potentialities of matter in a new light.

There are good scientific grounds for stressing the continuity of the physical with the biological world, so perhaps the cosmic process may be described as "materialistic," provided the term is understood in the light of this. However, the qualification of "materialistic" just made may, in the end, be so drastic that some other less misleading term becomes necessary. For "matter" appears to be far more subtle and its potentialities far richer and more diverse than can be inferred from observations made at any single particular level of the development of the cosmos, especially the simplest and least complex.

ON GOD

The postulate of God as Creator of all-that-is is not, in its most profound form, a statement about what happened at a particular point in time. To speak of God as Creator is a postulate about a perennial or "eternal"—that is to say, timeless—relation of God to the world, a relation that involves both differentiation and interaction. God is differentiated from the world in that he is totally other than it (indeed *this* dualism—of God and the world—is the only one that is foundational to Christian thought).

God is postulated in answer to the question, Why is there anything at all? He is the "Ground of Being" of the world or, for theists, that without which we could neither make sense of the world having existence at all nor of its having that kind of intellectually coherent and explorable existence that science continuously unveils.

This affirmation of what is termed "transcendence" has to be held in tension with the sense of God's immanence in the world. For if the world is in any sense created by God, and is that through which he acts and expresses his own being, then there is a sense in which God is never absent from the world. Nowadays science emphasizes more than ever before that creation is continuous (a *creatio continua*), and twentieth-century theists, even more than their predecessors, have come to see the ongoing cosmic processes of evolution as God himself creat*ing* in his own universe. The basic concept here is that all-that-is, both nature and human beings, is in some sense *in* God, but that God is more than nature and the human. God in his being transcends, goes beyond, both humankind and nature.

Either God is in everything created from the beginning to the end, at all times and in all places, or he is not there at all. What we see in the world is the mode of God's creativity in the world. God is in his world as Beethoven is in, say, his Seventh Symphony while it is being performed. In the actual processes of the world, and supremely in human consciousness, God is involving himself and expressing himself as Creator. However, since human beings have free will we have also to recognize that God puts himself "at risk," as it were, in creating in the natural world beings who can transcend their perceived world and shape it in their own way.

ON THE RELATIONSHIP BETWEEN NATURE, HUMAN BEINGS, AND GOD

In evolution there is an interplay between random chance at the micro level and the necessity that arises from the stuff of this world having its particular "given" properties. These potentialities a theist must regard as written into creation by the Creator himself. God as Creator we now see as somewhat like a composer who, beginning with an arrangement of notes in an apparently simple sequence, elaborates and expands it into a fugue by a variety of devices. In this way the Creator may be imagined to unfold the potentialities of the universe, which he himself put into it, selecting and shaping those that are to come to fruition.

The processes of the universe are continuous, and in them arise new organizations of matter-energy. Such new levels of organization require epistemologically nonreducible concepts to articulate their distinctiveness. Any new meaning that God thereby expresses is thus not discontinuous with the meanings expressed in that out of which it has emerged. *Both* continuity *and* emergence of the new are features inherent in the observed world. So we would anticipate continuity, with new meanings emerging out of the old, subsuming them, perhaps, but not denying them.

Now evolved human beings seek such meaning and intelligibility in the world; that is, from a theist's point of view, they seek to discern the meanings expressed by God in creation. These are meanings that, alone among created organisms, we are capable of both consciously discerning and freely appropriating to give purpose and meaning to our lives.

Although we should not regard God as more present at one time or place than at others, nevertheless, we should not be surprised to find that in some sequences of events in nature and history God unveils his meaning more clearly than in others. Though God as Creator acts in all events, not all events are equally *perceived* as "acts of God." Some events will reveal more to us than others. The aspect of God's meaning expressed by any one level in the natural hierarchy of complexity is limited to what it can itself distinctively convey, but how much we perceive of this depends on our sensitivity or responsiveness to that level.

Thus, although God must in his own being *ex hypothesi* be suprapersonal, we may well expect that in personal experience, personal encounter, and in human history, we shall find meanings of God unveiled in a way that we will not perceive through *im*personal events. For, the more personal and *self*-conscious the entity in which God is immanent, the more capable it is of expressing God's suprapersonal characteristics, and the more God can be immanent in that entity. The distinctive transcendence-in-immanence of human experience, furthermore, raises the hope among those who seek God in his created work that uniquely in a human being there might be unveiled, without distortion, the transcendent Creator who is immanent; that is to say, that in *a* human being (or beings) the presence of God the Creator might be revealed with a clarity not hitherto perceived.

It is the distinctive affirmation of *Christian* theists that this has actually happened—to Jews a stumbling block and to the Greeks foolishness;[21] to other religions a demeaning of the Almighty, Eternal One so to enter material existence; to the Western intellectual a unique, lawless surd, indeed, an absurdity in a law-abiding universe. Yet is it so antitheistic, is it so inconsistent with profounder trends and laws and with the concepts of God I have been elaborating to affirm that at a particular time and place in history, the God who had all along been immanent in the whole temporal creative process should have expressed himself directly, personally, and concretely in and through a particular person who, humanly speaking, was completely open to him? The effort to describe the nature of that person through whom God so revealed himself constituted a major transition in the way humankind came to think of nature, of God, and of itself. For it profoundly affected human perception of God, of human destiny, and of nature.

To take just the last, human understanding of nature was gradually transformed in Christian consciousness because, if God was able to express his nature—that is, "incarnate" himself—in a human being, then the world of matter organized in the form we call human must inherently be capable of thus being a vehicle of God's action and of expressing God's being. This in itself constituted a repudiation of the attitudes of all who saw the stuff of the world as evil, alien to its Creator, a prison from which a non-material reason, or "soul," must seek release. God must henceforth be seen as achieving his ends by involvement with, immanence in, expression through, the very stuff of the world and its events in space and time. Moreover, the assertion that Jesus the Christ was the ultimate revelation of God's being in a mode that human beings could understand and appropriate amounted to an affirmation that nature in its actuality, materiality, and evolution, of which Jesus was indubitably a part, is, potentially, at least, both an expression of God's being and the instrument of his action. Paradoxically, the Christian claim asserts that God fulfills human personalness, and satisfies humankind's highest aspirations, by entering the temporal process as a person, made like all human beings of the component units of the stuff of the world.

There is indeed a *Christian* materialism. As David Jenkins put it in his Bampton lectures:

The Christian discovery on the basis of the givenness of Jesus Christ was that man and the universe hold together because of the involvement of God to that end. Thus materiality and history provide the stuff for the attainment of ultimate reality and the fulfilment of absolute value.[22]

In the introduction, I quoted William Temple's dictum concerning Christianity as the most materialistic of all great religions. Now I can make clear why he said that. In his own words:

It may safely be said that one ground for the hope of Christianity that it may make good its claim to be the true faith lies in the fact that it is the most avowedly materialist of all the great religions. It affords an expectation that it may be able to control the material, precisely because it does not ignore it or deny it, but roundly asserts alike the reality of matter and its subordination. Its own most central saying is: "The Word was made flesh," where the last term was, no doubt, chosen because of its specially materialistic associations. By the very nature of its central doctrine Christianity is committed to a belief in the ultimate significance of the historical process, and in the reality of matter and its place in the divine scheme.[23]

Furthermore, there is in the long tradition of Christian thought, going back to Jesus' own actions and words, a way of relating the physical and the personal worlds that avoids any stark dichotomy between them, seeing them as two facets of the same reality. This way of thinking is generally denoted by the word *sacramental*. In the

Christian liturgy, things in the universe—bread, wine, water, oil sometimes—are taken as being both symbols of God's self-expression and instruments of God's action in effecting his purposes.

This mode of thinking can be extended to the universe as a whole, which can then be seen as both a symbol of God's self-expression, and thus a mode of his revelation of himself, and also the very means whereby he effects his purposes in his own actions as agent.[24] It provides, I think, a deeper perspective on the world described by the sciences than the sciences alone can afford, a perspective in which the world's continuous and seamless web of development, of self-organizing by its own inherent properties, generates forms of matter, that is, persons, that are capable of perceiving meaning—those meanings, indeed, with which the Creator imbued his creation.

In this chapter, I have addressed myself to what to many may seem the paradox of linking the Christian perspective with "materialism." I hope the question mark in my title at least indicates that the word *materialism* has to be taken in a somewhat Pickwickian sense—and certainly not in that of nineteenth-century materialists. Far from any reduction to the material being intended, the juxtaposition of the adjective *Christian* and the noun *materialism* seeks to highlight the significance of the stuff of the world, its *matter* as we normally call it, but now including energy within this term. This significance lies in the potentialities of that world-stuff, potentialities that have been expounded in the previous chapters showing how that stuff can become intelligent and display cognitive abilities. I hope that what I have said will also be heard as a plea for a serious consideration of the Christian perspective as a total worldview that can incorporate without fear, and be open to, the fascinating explorations into the nature of the human by the cognitive and other sciences.

What I have said is also intended as a plea for the humanities. It is my conviction that Christianity is committed to a *Christian* humanism in the tradition of Erasmus and of the Florentine Renaissance (though we cannot go into that now). My principal plea is more general, namely, that if, as Alexander Pope said, the "proper study of mankind" is indeed "man," then the study of human rational intelligence—in its choice making, assessment of the consequences of action, abstract conceptualization, all its cognitive functions—is attending to only the echo of a whisper of a hint of a rumor of that incessant inner and outer dialogue that constitutes the essence of human self-awareness. To learn about *that,* we must sit at the feet of the poets, dramatists, novelists, artists, dancers, sculptors, composers, and men and women of God.

In brief, our culture needs not only information and information technology, it needs, above all, wisdom. Science has, of course, its own style of down-to-earth wisdom, removing the layers of accummulated prejudice, and at the Twentieth Nobel Conference we heard how its own powerful methods have begun to shed their own particular kind of light on that great mystery, How do we know? However, the cognitive sciences should not in the end be divorced from the great stream of human experience expressed through the rich resources of language, music, and symbol that we receive from the past and that continues today. As Socrates *might* have said,

Until humanists are cognitive scientists or the cognitive scientists and computer experts of this world have the spirit and power of the humanities, and computing greatness and wisdom meet in one, and those commoner natures who pursue either to the exclusion of the other are compelled to stand aside, cities will never have rest from their evils—no, nor the human race, as I believe—and then only will this our State have a possibility of life and behold the light of day.[25]

DISCUSSION

Q: *Would you say that God without the world is nevertheless God, or would you say that God without the world is not God?*

A: I believe that William Temple said something on this that is interesting: "God minus the world equals God; but the world minus God equals nothing."

One of the reasons orthodox, classical ideas tend to be at the center of our thinking is probably that there are many reasons for them within a certain framework. The idea here is that any God worth worshiping must not in the end make his existence dependent on that of which he is the Creator. This is the trouble with process theology in my view: It makes a captive God. Was it Dorothy Sayers who said that the bother with the God of process theology was that, if you want to worship him, you need to pity him?

I think that if there is any basic concept of deity, an *x* that is the ground of being, that gives being to all that is, then that being is not in the long run dependent upon the existence of anything else, except that the hypothesis, the idea itself, involves the urge within that being to create—rather like the artist's urge to create. I think that is why one of the best models of God is drawn from the artistic and aesthetic analogies. So that is why we have the equation, "God minus the world equals God."

The other equation is really very Thomistic: "The world minus God equals nothing." This is a brief way of stating the classical idea that Thomas spelled out very cogently in the *Summa*, namely, that any doctrine of creation involves the concept that what is created is given by God. Its existence is dependent upon God, and without God it would not be at all. This is the sense of God's supporting and preserving and giving being to all that is, so that "the world minus God equals nothing."

That is a short, succinct summary of fifteen hundred years of profound thought.

NOTES

1. Leo Tolstoy, *The Death of Iván Ilích, and Other Stories,* trans. L. and H. Maude (London: World's Classics, Oxford University Press, 1971), pp. 44, 45.
2. Alexander Pope, *An Essay on Man,* 2.15 (1733).
3. John Donne, *An Anatomy of the World,* 1.205.
4. William Temple, *Readings in St. John's Gospel,* (London: Macmillan, 1955), pp. xx, xxi.
5. William Temple, *Nature, Man and God* (London: Macmillan, 1964; 1st ed. 1934).
6. F. J. Ayala, in Intro. to *Studies in the Philosophy of Biology: Reduction and Related Problems,* ed. F. J. Ayala & T. Dobzhansky (London: Macmillan, 1974), p. ix.
7. Francis H. C. Crick, *Of Molecules and Man* (Seattle: University of Washington Press, 1966), p. 10.
8. P. Medawar, "A Geometric Model of Reduction and Emergence," in Ayala and Dobzhansky, *Studies in the Philosophy of Biology,* p. 61; F. Jacob, *The Logic of Living Systems* (London: Allen Lane, 1974), "Biology can neither be reduced to physics, nor do without it," p. 302.
9. W. C. Wimsatt, "Robustness, Reliability and Over-determination," in *Scientific Inquiry and the Social Sciences,* ed. M. Brewer and B. Collins (San Francisco: Jossey-Bass, 1981), pp. 124–63.
10. Genesis 3:19.
11. H. Wheeler Robinson, "Hebrew Psychology," in *The People and the Book,* ed. A. S. Peake (Oxford: Clarendon Press, 1925), p. 362.

12. W. Eichrodt, *Theology of the New Testament*, trans. J. A. Baker (London: SCM Press, 1967), vol. 2, p. 124. He expounds this subsequently in the following terms: "Of the greatest consequence, however, is the realism in biblical psychology, which brings the body into organic connection with the psychic life. . . . For the body is not an object which we possess, but which stands outside our real being; it is not simply the natural basis and instrument to which we are assigned, but which does not belong to our essential self. It is the living form of that self, the necessary expression of our individual existence, in which the meaning of our life must find its realization. . . . it is understood as in all its parts the medium of a spiritual and personal life, which stands under divine vocation, and finds its nobility in being God's image" (p. 149).

13. J. A. Baker has stressed both the "earthiness" and the personal aspects of the Hebrew view, which he expounds as follows: "Man is formed of matter. His every thought, feeling, action, his most transcendental conceptions, have their origin in, and are made possible by, the same basic particles as those from which the whole cosmos is built. It is through the body, therefore, that man has to live. . . . But the paradox of man's being is that, though he is thus physical through and through, he is also something much more—a non-physical reality, a person. This truth is bound up with his self-awareness, which is of such a kind that he can address himself as 'thou.' . . . This personhood is a different kind of fact from the fact of his body; indeed, it is the determinative, classifying fact about him" ("Man: His Nature, Predicament and Hope, [1] The Old Testament," in *Man: Fallen and Free*, ed. E. W. Kemp (London: Hodder & Stoughton, 1969], p. 94).

14. The contrast in some Pauline passages of *sarx* ("flesh") and *pneuma* ("spirit") is not, as is commonly believed, that of body, conceived as evil, as against disembodied and eternal soul, conceived as good. For *sarx* possesses psychical attributes and refers rather to the human being's total created nature in its weakness, by contrast with and distant from God, whereas *pneuma* is that by virtue of which human beings are open and sensitive to the life of God. Living *kata sarka* ("after, or according to, the flesh") denotes wrong living, not because matter or the body are in any way evil, but because living in this manner is living for the world and not for God and is thus a distortion of the human relationship with God.

See also, in this context, I. T. Ramsey's account of Pauline anthropology together with an interpretation of the meaning of "soul" that takes into consideration current scientific knowledge: "There is for St. Paul, at least in theory, the natural man, the man who is nothing but a combined topic of the natural and behavioural sciences, who receiveth not the things of the Spirit of God (I Corinthians 2:14), whose life is restricted to the natural world; the man who in one sense does not live as distinct from existing. But there is by contrast the 'spiritual man' who discerns the things of the Spirit of God, who (we may alternatively translate) is braced by the wind of God blowing in his face, who realizes himself as he responds to the activity of God disclosed in Christ, who 'sees' the deep things of God, the activities of God known in a situation of depth. Here is the spiritual man, defined by a specific kind of activity—the basic personality matrix which he realizes as he responds to the gospel—who finds his life and freedom in responding to what he discerns in depth. Here is the man who in theological terms is saved and made whole and who, under the inspiration of the haunting vision of the gospel, can pioneer whatever changes come to man or society as scientific exploration takes us further into unknown and exciting terrain. He goes forward in faith, confident that under the inspiration of his vision there can be a creative outcome to the travail in which we endeavour to match medico-scientific developments with the needs and possibilities of human life and society.

"Here, then, in a personality which each of us discovers in an active self-response to a disclosure of God's activity in Christ, is for the Christian that which unifies, that which is distinctive of each of us. This is that to which the word 'soul' was meant to point; that which can be expressed in directed thought or bodily activity. Here is no metaphysical substructure or pin-cushion, no static centre, but that which we know in being active, in realizing ourselves. Here is the permanent complement of all scientific discourse, something implicit in all the strands of knowledge with which the natural and behavioural sciences supply us" (I. T. Ramsey, "Human Personality," in *Personality and Science: An Interdisciplinary Discussion*, ed. I. T. Ramsey and R. Potter [Edinburgh & London: Churchill-Livingstone, 1971], p. 130–31).

15. Eichrodt, *Theology of the New Testament*, p. 126.

16. Cf. D. Wiggins, "Identity-Statements," in *Analytical Philosophy, Second Series*, ed. R. J. Butler (Oxford: Blackwell, 1965), p. 41.

17. S. Kripke, "Naming and Necessity," in *Semantics of Natural Language*, 2d ed., ed. G. Harman and D. Davidson (Dordrecht: Reidel, 1972), pp. 253–355.

18. D. Davidson, "Mental Events," in *Experience and Theory*, ed. L. Foster and J. W. Swanson (Amherst: University of Massachusetts Press, 1970).

19. Cf. J. A. Fodor, in *Psychological Explanations* (New York: Random House, 1968), chap. 3; and D. Davidson, "Mental Events."

20. I. T. Ramsey, "Human Personality," p. 127–28.

21. 1 Corinthians 1:23.

22. D. E. Jenkins, *The Glory of Man* (London: SCM Press, 1967), p. 53 ff. Jenkins continues: "Jesus Christ, because he is a man, is, like every other man, continuous as a physical organism with the whole of the rest of the universe. There is no more of an evolutionary break between the cooling of a spiral nebula and the man Jesus than there is in the case of any one of us. Between the cosmic dust and us there is no discontinuity. So Jesus Christ is all that is involved in being man including the possibility of analytical reduction to whatever are the units of the stuff of the universe. . . . In the purposes of the transcendent and independent God, and by the power of this God, a union has been achieved between that evolutionary product of cosmic dust which is a human being and that transcendent and wholly other purposeful personalness who is God. Transcendent and independent personalness is at one with derived, dependent and evolved personality whose whole basis can be reduced to that impersonal materiality out of which it has developed and on which it depends."

23. William Temple, *Nature, Man and God*, p. 478.

24. Cf. William Temple, "It is clear that . . . we are trying to frame a conception which is not identical with any of the commonly offered suggestions concerning the relation of the eternal and the historical, and are now extending its application so as to include the relation of the spiritual and material. It is not simply the relation of ground and consequent, nor of cause and effect, nor of thoughts and expression, nor of purpose and instrument, nor of end and means, but it is all of these at once. We need for it another name; and there is in some religious traditions an element which is, in the belief of adherent of those religions, so close akin to what we want that we may most suitably call this conception of the relation of the eternal to history, of spirit to matter, the sacramental conception" (*Nature, Man and God*, pp. 481–82).

25. Cf. Plato, *Republic*, 5.

Afterword: The Brain-in-a-Box

MICHAEL SHAFTO

Something Roger Schank said at the Nobel Conference reminded me of a course I once took at a small college near Gustavus. The course was popular because it satisfied several distribution requirements. It was cross-listed in history, physics, and philosophy. The name of the course was "Possible Worlds"; it was a survey course. Its only drawback was that it required a lot of reading.

As a student in "Possible Worlds," I wrote a term paper about a possible world very similar to our own. The only fundamental difference between my world and ours was that in my world the history of science had been slightly altered. Galileo, Newton, and Einstein were all biologists. (Darwin was attacked by reactionaries because of his views on astronomy.) To make a long story short, in my world biology was a much more advanced science than physics, and, in particular, John von Neumann was a biochemist.

This perturbation of the history of science had some interesting consequences for the development of technology. In my world, von Neumann, the biochemist, invented the first practical, general-purpose, stored-program computer. But this von Neumann machine was quite different from our digital computers. In fact, it was never called a computer, because it was not particularly good at computing.

Its structure and function reflected von Neumann's biochemical genius. It became known colloquially as the Brain-in-a-Box. This name was shortened to "B'n'B," and finally to "BB."

At first the BB was a mere curiosity. To get one to do anything moderately interesting, you had to get it adopted by an expert who was willing to tutor it for about ten years. Eventually, by using specially designed BBs to do the tutoring, it was possible to cut the training time in half. This automatic training procedure, or incremental resonance modulation, as it was called by technicians, was ungainly, and it never became highly reliable. "Empty" BBs had to be arranged in a rectangular array. There might be thirty to sixty of them, all neatly arranged by rank and file. They were all connected to the same tutorial BB, which had to be preprogrammed with some sort of knowledge. The tutorial BB would then transmit signals to the "empty" BBs in an attempt to "fill them up" with the appropriate knowledge. Naturally, there was appreciable noise in this type of training system. It was, however, more cost-effective than having a single tutor for each individual BB.

Practical problems besieged the BB-training effort from every side: Because of their complex biochemical structure, BBs required some fairly expensive, hard-to-synthesize nutrients. They also required careful temperature control. If they dropped below 90 degrees Fahrenheit, they had to be scrapped or converted into missile guidance systems. If they heated up to 106 degrees Fahrenheit, they became "neutralized" and could only be used as nondirective psychotherapists. They had to be shut down completely for eight hours a day. Perhaps for this reason, they never showed much aptitude for difficult subjects like science and math (especially proofs).

Nevertheless, BBs (with suitable prostheses and interfacing) proved reasonably skillful at pattern recognition, mundane reasoning, and natural language, though they preferred not to speak in front of large groups. Commercially produced BBs became able to take over simple jobs, replacing accountants, airline counter personnel, and many middle-level managers. There was a mild panic when someone circulated a rumor, apparently unfounded, that they were planning to unionize.

After BBs had been around for a decade or two, there coalesced a small group of psychologists and philosophers who suggested that BBs were somewhat like human beings. These maverick intellectuals pointed out that, although BBs were artifacts, they could learn, reason, converse, and find gainful employment, just like human beings. (It should be carefully noted that biologists, who understood the nitty-gritty details of BB-engineering, were never to be found among these fuzzy-thinking radicals.)

Of course, these exaggerated claims drew howls of derision from critics. Could you really call it *learning* when BBs required at least five years to get up to speed in any halfway challenging subject? When they had to be explicitly trained to do even simple tasks like market analysis? When, even if they managed to get the right answer, they usually couldn't explain how they did it? When they had almost no taste for art or literature? When they had less imagination than the average dolphin?

Besides, despite their colloquial name, they didn't even look like real brains. They looked like boxes of lumpy gravy with tympani sticks suspended in it. And the box was square, not round. How could a box of gravy support symbolic thought?

The critics wanted some evidence of real intelligence, some kind of performance that was less mundane, something really impressive: memorizing an entire phone book, proving a theorem in topology, working through a complicated logic problem *really fast*, or playing a decent game of chess. The critics pointed to the work of a couple of young engineers named Watson and Crick, who had rigged up a gizmo out of wires and light bulbs that could add two big numbers in a fraction of a second. Now there, said the critics, was an idea with some real potential.